Creative Mind and Success

Self-Discovery, Exploring Creativity, and Realising Your Full Potential

Creative Mind and Success

Self-Discovery, Exploring Creativity, and Realising Your Full Potential

ISHI MACAY

The Readers Paradise
New Delhi - 110002

Creative Mind and Success
Ishi Macay

ISBN - 978-93-5977-865-5

Published by The Readers Paradise
www.thereadersparadise.com

Printed and bound by CPI Group (UK) Ltd, Croydon, CR0 4YY

Cover Design by Kamini Bijoria

Typeset by The Readers Paradise

First Edition: 2024

MIX
Paper | Supporting responsible forestry
FSC® C171272
FSC www.fsc.org

Preface

Welcome to "Creative Mind and Success: Self-Discovery, Exploring Creativity, and Realising Your Full Potential." This book is your guide to unlocking the immense power of creativity within you and harnessing it to achieve personal and professional success. Creativity is not just the realm of artists and musicians; it is a fundamental aspect of human potential that can transform every area of your life.

In today's fast-paced world, the ability to think creatively is more important than ever. Whether you're an entrepreneur, a corporate professional, a student, or someone seeking personal growth, creativity can provide the tools you need to innovate, solve problems, and navigate the complexities of modern life. This book aims to demystify creativity, showing you that it's a skill that can be cultivated and applied to every facet of your life.

Know Your Mind

We begin our journey with a deep dive into understanding your mind. Knowing how your mind works is the first step in unlocking your creative potential. In this section, we explore the importance of creativity in modern life and how it fuels success across various fields. You will learn the crucial steps to take your ideas from inception to execution, understanding the distinct functions of the left and right brain. We will also delve into the growth mindset versus the fixed mindset, providing strategies to cultivate a positive and productive mindset that embraces challenges and fosters continuous learning.

Understand Creativity

Next, we demystify creativity itself. What does it truly mean to be creative? We will define creativity and dispel common myths and misconceptions. You'll discover the science behind creative thinking and how you can leverage it to enhance your innovation capabilities. This section also highlights the power of creative collaboration and the importance of building a network of like-minded individuals who can support and inspire your creative endeavours.

Are You Creative?

Everyone has the potential to be creative. In this section, we help you measure your creativity and explore the different types of creativity that exist. Whether your creativity lies in artistic expression, problem-solving, or strategic thinking, you will learn to recognise and nurture your unique creative strengths.

Unleashing Your Creative Potential

This is where the magic happens. We provide practical techniques to stimulate creative thinking and identify and overcome mental blocks that hinder your creative flow. You will learn daily habits that nurture creativity and strategies for creative problem-solving in everyday situations. Additionally, we explore how creativity can enhance personal relationships, the benefits of creative hobbies, and how to foster a creative environment at work. You'll also discover how innovative thinking can advance your career and how to find and follow your passion. Building resilience and staying motivated are essential parts of the creative journey, and we provide insights and techniques to help you maintain your creative momentum.

Case Studies

Real-world examples are powerful tools for learning. This section features case studies of individuals and organisations that have successfully harnessed creativity to achieve remarkable success. These stories will inspire and provide practical insights into applying creative principles in your own life.

Activities on Fostering Creativity

Finally, we offer a range of activities designed to foster creativity. These exercises are fun, engaging, and designed to help you think outside the box, collaborate with others, and continually develop your creative skills.

"Creative Mind and Success" is more than just a book; it's a toolkit for transforming your life. By understanding and harnessing the power of your creative mind, you can achieve your full potential and find success and fulfillment in all areas of your life. So, embark on this journey with an open mind and a willingness to explore, and let your creativity lead the way to success.

Welcome to your creative journey. Let's begin.

Contents

1

The Importance of Creativity in Modern Life

In today's fast-paced and ever-changing world, creativity has become more crucial than ever before. From solving complex problems to developing innovative products, creativity is at the heart of modern life. But what exactly is creativity, and why is it so important? In this chapter, we'll explore the significance of creativity in contemporary society and how it can be nurtured to achieve success.

Understanding Creativity

Creativity is the ability to generate new ideas, solutions, or possibilities that are valuable and unique. It involves thinking outside the box, challenging conventional wisdom, and seeing things from different perspectives. Creativity isn't limited to the arts; it's equally vital in science, business, education, and everyday life. Whether you're an artist painting a masterpiece, a scientist developing a new theory, or a manager solving a workplace issue, creativity is the driving force behind innovation and progress.

The Role of Creativity in Problem-Solving

One of the most significant roles of creativity is in problem-solving. In modern life, we constantly face challenges that require innovative solutions. Traditional methods may not always work, and this is where creativity comes into play. Creative thinking allows us to approach problems from different angles, consider various possibilities, and come up with effective solutions. This ability is particularly important in the workplace, where problems can be complex and multifaceted. A creative mind can see opportunities where others see obstacles and can turn challenges into successes.

Innovation and Progress

Innovation is the engine of progress, and creativity is the fuel that powers it. Every new invention, technology, or advancement starts with a creative idea. From the invention of the wheel to the development of the internet, creativity has driven human progress throughout history. In today's technology-driven world, innovation is happening at an unprecedented pace, and creativity is more important than ever. Companies that foster creativity are at the forefront of innovation, creating products and services that shape the future. Encouraging creativity in the workplace not only leads to new ideas but also keeps businesses competitive and relevant in a rapidly changing market.

Creativity in the Workplace

In the modern workplace, creativity is a highly sought-after skill. Employers value creative employees who can think critically, solve problems, and contribute to innovation. A creative workforce is more adaptable, resilient, and capable of driving growth. Encouraging creativity at work can lead to increased job satisfaction and employee engagement. When employees feel that their ideas are valued and that they have the freedom to think creatively, they are more motivated and productive. Moreover, a creative work environment fosters collaboration and teamwork, as people come together to share ideas and build on each other's creativity.

Education and Creativity

Education plays a crucial role in nurturing creativity. Traditional education systems have often focused on rote learning and standardised testing, which can stifle creative thinking. However, there is a growing recognition of the importance of fostering creativity in schools. Creative education encourages students to explore their interests, think independently, and develop their unique talents. By incorporating creative activities into the curriculum, such as art, music, drama, and creative writing, schools can help students develop critical thinking and problem-solving skills. Moreover, creative education prepares students for the future, equipping them with the skills needed to thrive in a rapidly changing world.

Everyday Creativity

Creativity isn't just for artists, scientists, or business leaders; it's a valuable skill for everyone in everyday life. From cooking a meal to decorating a home, we all engage in creative activities that enrich our lives. Everyday creativity helps us to express ourselves, solve daily problems, and find joy in the little things. It also enhances our mental well-being, providing an outlet for stress and a means of personal fulfilment. By nurturing our creative side, we can lead more balanced, fulfilling lives and face life's challenges with a positive and open mindset.

Overcoming Barriers to Creativity

Despite its importance, creativity can often be stifled by various barriers. Fear of failure, criticism, and rigid thinking are some of the common obstacles that hinder creative expression. To overcome these barriers, it's important to create an environment that fosters creativity. Encouraging risk-taking, embracing failure as a learning opportunity, and promoting open-mindedness can help unleash creativity. Additionally, setting aside time for creative activities and allowing for mental breaks can boost creative thinking. It's also helpful to surround yourself with diverse perspectives and experiences, as this can inspire new ideas and ways of thinking.

Creativity and Personal Growth

Creativity plays a vital role in personal growth and development. Engaging in creative activities helps us to explore our interests, develop new skills, and discover our potential. It also encourages self-reflection and personal insight, helping us to understand ourselves better. By nurturing our creativity, we can achieve a sense of accomplishment and fulfilment that contributes to overall well-being. Whether it's through painting, writing, gardening, or any other creative pursuit, taking time for creativity can lead to a richer, more meaningful life.

The Future of Creativity

As we look to the future, creativity will continue to be a driving force in shaping our world. In an age of automation and artificial intelligence, human creativity is what will set us apart. While machines can perform repetitive tasks, they lack the ability to think creatively and innovate. This makes creativity a uniquely human skill that will be increasingly valuable in the future. By nurturing creativity in ourselves and others, we can ensure that we remain at the forefront of innovation and progress.

Practical Tips for Enhancing Creativity

To tap into your creative potential, here are some practical tips:

1. **Stay Curious**: Ask questions, explore new interests, and never stop learning. Curiosity is the spark that ignites creativity.
2. **Embrace Failure**: Don't be afraid to fail. Every failure is a learning opportunity that brings you closer to success.
3. **Take Breaks**: Give your mind time to rest and recharge. Taking breaks can lead to new insights and ideas.
4. **Surround Yourself with Creativity**: Engage with creative people, visit museums, read books, and expose yourself to different forms of art.
5. **Practice Mindfulness**: Mindfulness practices, such as meditation, can help clear your mind and enhance creative thinking.
6. **Set Aside Time for Creativity**: Dedicate time each day for creative activities, whether it's drawing, writing, or simply brainstorming.
7. **Be Open to New Experiences**: Try new things, travel, and embrace diverse perspectives. New experiences can inspire fresh ideas.
8. **Keep a Journal**: Write down your thoughts, ideas, and observations. A journal can be a valuable tool for capturing and developing creative ideas.
9. **Collaborate with Others**: Share your ideas and work with others. Collaboration can lead to new perspectives and innovative solutions.
10. **Stay Positive**: Maintain a positive attitude and believe in your creative abilities. Confidence is key to unlocking creativity.

Creativity is an essential skill in modern life that drives innovation, solves problems, and enriches our lives. By nurturing creativity in ourselves and others, we can achieve personal growth, professional success, and a more fulfilling life. Remember, creativity is not a rare talent reserved for a few; it's a skill that everyone can develop and enjoy. So, embrace your creative potential and let it guide you towards a brighter and more innovative future.

2

How Creativity Fuels Success

Creativity is often seen as the spark that ignites success. Whether in business, personal development, or everyday life, creativity plays a pivotal role in helping us achieve our goals and dreams. In this chapter, we will delve into how creativity fuels success, exploring its impact on problem-solving, innovation, leadership, and personal growth. By understanding the importance of creativity, we can harness its power to unlock our full potential and achieve remarkable success.

Creativity and Problem-Solving

Creativity is at the heart of effective problem-solving. In our daily lives, we encounter numerous challenges that require innovative solutions. Traditional approaches may not always work, and that's where creative thinking becomes essential. Creative problem-solving involves looking at a problem from different angles, thinking outside the box, and generating unique ideas. This approach enables us to find effective and often unexpected solutions that can lead to success.

In the workplace, creative problem-solving is highly valued. Employers seek individuals who can tackle complex issues with innovative solutions. When faced with a challenge, a creative thinker can come up with multiple alternatives, assess their feasibility, and implement the best one. This ability to think creatively not only resolves immediate problems but also contributes to long-term success by fostering a culture of continuous improvement and adaptability.

Innovation and Competitive Advantage

Innovation is a key driver of success in today's competitive world, and creativity is the engine that powers it. Innovative ideas and products can set businesses apart from their competitors, leading to market leadership and sustained growth. Creativity enables individuals and organisations to develop new products, services, and processes that meet evolving customer needs and preferences. By fostering a culture of creativity, businesses can stay ahead of the curve and maintain a competitive edge.

In addition to driving business success, innovation fueled by creativity can lead to personal success. Creative individuals often find unique ways to stand out in their careers, whether by developing new skills, offering fresh perspectives, or creating novel solutions. This innovative mindset can open doors to new opportunities, promotions, and career advancement. By continuously seeking creative ways to improve and innovate, individuals can achieve remarkable success and fulfilment in their professional lives.

Leadership and Vision

Effective leadership is closely linked to creativity. Great leaders are often visionary thinkers who can see beyond the present and imagine a better future. They use their creativity to inspire and motivate others, develop innovative strategies, and navigate through challenges. Creative leaders are not afraid to take risks, embrace change, and think differently. This ability to envision and drive change is crucial for achieving long-term success in any organisation.

Moreover, creativity in leadership fosters a positive and dynamic work environment. Creative leaders encourage their teams to think creatively, share ideas, and collaborate. This collaborative atmosphere leads to a more engaged and motivated workforce, which in turn drives higher performance and success. By valuing and promoting creativity, leaders can unlock the full potential of their teams and achieve outstanding results.

Personal Growth and Fulfilment

Creativity plays a significant role in personal growth and fulfilment. Engaging in creative activities allows individuals to explore their interests, develop new skills, and express themselves. This process of self-discovery and development is essential for achieving personal success. Whether through art, writing, music, or any other creative pursuit, individuals can find joy and satisfaction in their creative endeavours, leading to a more fulfilling and balanced life.

Furthermore, creativity helps individuals overcome personal challenges and setbacks. When faced with difficulties, creative thinking enables individuals to find new perspectives and solutions. This resilience and adaptability are crucial for personal success, as they allow individuals to navigate through life's ups and downs with confidence and optimism. By nurturing their creative side, individuals can build a strong foundation for personal growth and long-term success.

Building Strong Relationships

Creativity also plays a vital role in building strong and

meaningful relationships. Creative communication and problem-solving skills can enhance interactions with others, leading to deeper connections and mutual understanding. Whether in personal or professional relationships, creativity helps individuals find common ground, resolve conflicts, and collaborate effectively. These strong relationships are essential for achieving success, as they provide support, inspiration, and opportunities for growth.

In the workplace, creative collaboration fosters a sense of teamwork and camaraderie. When individuals bring their unique ideas and perspectives to the table, it leads to more innovative and effective solutions. This collaborative spirit not only drives project success but also contributes to a positive and productive work environment. By valuing and encouraging creativity in their interactions, individuals can build strong relationships that support their success and well-being.

Enhancing Mental Well-Being

Engaging in creative activities has a positive impact on mental well-being, which is a crucial factor in achieving success. Creativity provides an outlet for self-expression and stress relief, helping individuals manage their emotions and maintain a healthy mindset. Whether through painting, writing, or playing an instrument, creative activities offer a therapeutic escape from the pressures of daily life. This mental clarity and emotional balance are essential for maintaining focus, productivity, and overall success.

Moreover, creativity promotes a growth mindset, encouraging individuals to embrace challenges and view failures as learning opportunities. This positive attitude towards personal development fosters resilience and perseverance, key traits for achieving success. By incorporating creativity into their daily routines, individuals can enhance their mental well-being and build a strong foundation for personal and professional success.

Practical Tips for Fostering Creativity

To harness the power of creativity and fuel success, here are some practical tips:

1. **Create a Stimulating Environment**: Surround yourself with inspiring materials, such as books, art, and music. A stimulating environment can spark new ideas and enhance creative thinking.
2. **Take Risks and Experiment**: Don't be afraid to try new things and take risks. Experimentation can lead to unexpected discoveries and breakthroughs.
3. **Stay Curious**: Cultivate a sense of curiosity and wonder. Ask questions, seek out new experiences, and never stop learning.
4. **Collaborate with Others**: Engage with people who have different perspectives and skills. Collaboration can lead to innovative solutions and new ideas.
5. **Set Aside Time for Creativity**: Dedicate regular time for creative activities, whether it's brainstorming, doodling, or exploring a new hobby. Consistent practice can enhance your creative skills.
6. **Embrace Failure**: View failures as learning opportunities rather than setbacks. Embracing failure can boost your confidence and encourage creative risk-taking.
7. **Practice Mindfulness**: Mindfulness practices, such as meditation, can clear your mind and enhance your focus, allowing for more creative thinking.
8. **Keep a Journal**: Write down your thoughts, ideas, and observations. A journal can help you track your creative progress and develop new insights.

9. **Explore Different Mediums**: Experiment with various creative mediums, such as painting, writing, or music. Exploring different forms of creativity can inspire new ideas and approaches.
10. **Stay Positive**: Maintain a positive attitude and believe in your creative potential. Confidence and optimism are key to unlocking creativity and achieving success.

Creativity is a powerful catalyst for success in all areas of life. From problem-solving and innovation to leadership and personal growth, creativity fuels our ability to achieve our goals and dreams. By fostering a creative mindset and incorporating creative practices into our daily lives, we can unlock our full potential and pave the way for remarkable success. Remember, creativity is not a rare talent reserved for a few; it's a skill that everyone can develop and enjoy. Embrace your creativity and let it guide you towards a successful and fulfilling future.

3

From Idea to Execution: Steps to Take

Transforming an idea into a successful reality is a journey that requires careful planning, determination, and creativity. Whether you're starting a new business, launching a project, or pursuing a personal goal, the process from idea to execution involves several crucial steps. In this chapter, we will explore these steps in detail, providing practical guidance to help you bring your ideas to life and achieve success.

1. Generating and Refining the Idea

The journey begins with generating and refining your idea. Inspiration can come from anywhere – a problem that needs solving, a gap in the market, or a personal passion. Start by brainstorming and jotting down all your thoughts. Don't worry about feasibility at this stage; the goal is to generate as many ideas as possible. Use mind maps, lists, or sketches to visualise your ideas and explore different angles.

Once you have a pool of ideas, it's time to refine them. Evaluate each idea based on its potential impact, feasibility, and alignment with your goals. Consider the resources you have, the market demand, and the possible challenges. Select the idea that stands out as the most promising and align it with your vision and objectives. This refinement process helps you focus on a clear and achievable goal.

2. Conducting Research

With a refined idea, the next step is conducting thorough research. Research helps you understand the market, identify your target audience, and uncover potential obstacles. Start by gathering information on your industry, competitors, and market trends. Look for gaps that your idea can fill and analyse how similar ideas have succeeded or failed.

In addition to market research, seek feedback from potential users or customers. Conduct surveys, interviews, or focus groups to gain insights into their needs and preferences. This feedback is invaluable for refining your idea further and ensuring it meets the expectations of your target audience. Comprehensive research provides a solid foundation for developing a viable plan and reducing risks.

3. Planning and Goal Setting

Effective planning and goal setting are crucial for turning your idea into reality. Begin by outlining the steps needed to execute your idea. Break down the process into manageable tasks and create a timeline. This roadmap will guide you through the execution phase and keep you on track. Set specific, measurable, achievable, relevant, and time-bound (SMART) goals to ensure clarity and focus.

Prioritise your tasks and allocate resources accordingly. Consider what tools, skills, and support you need to achieve your goals. Establish milestones to track your progress and celebrate small wins along the way. A well-structured plan not only provides direction but also motivates you to stay committed to your idea.

4. Building a Team

Depending on the scale of your idea, you may need to build a team to help you execute it. Surround yourself with people who have complementary skills and share your vision. Look for individuals who bring diverse perspectives and strengths to the table. A strong team can enhance creativity, problem-solving, and overall execution.

When building your team, clearly define roles and responsibilities. Ensure everyone understands the goals and their contributions towards achieving them. Foster open communication and collaboration to maintain a positive and productive working environment. A cohesive team can overcome challenges more effectively and drive the project towards success.

5. Developing a Prototype or Pilot

Creating a prototype or pilot is an essential step in bringing your idea to life. This preliminary version allows you to test and refine your concept before a full-scale launch. Depending on your idea, a prototype could be a physical model, a digital simulation, or a small-scale implementation. The goal is to identify any flaws, gather feedback, and make necessary improvements.

Testing your prototype provides valuable insights into its functionality and user experience. Engage with your target audience to get their feedback and observe how they interact with your product or service. Use this feedback to make adjustments and enhancements. A well-developed prototype increases the chances of a successful launch by ensuring your idea is practical and well-received.

6. Securing Funding and Resources

Executing your idea often requires funding and resources. Identify the financial and material resources needed to bring your idea to fruition. This may include funding for development, marketing, and operations. Explore various funding options, such as personal savings, loans, investors, or crowdfunding. Each option has its pros and cons, so choose the one that best suits your needs and circumstances.

In addition to funding, secure the resources needed for execution. This includes tools, technology, workspace, and any other materials essential for your project. Establish a budget to manage expenses and ensure efficient use of resources. Proper financial planning and resource management are crucial for the successful execution of your idea.

7. Launching and Marketing

The launch phase is an exciting yet challenging step in the journey from idea to execution. Plan your launch carefully to create maximum impact. Choose the right time and platform for your launch, considering your target audience and market conditions. Develop a marketing strategy to create awareness and generate interest in your product or service.

Utilise various marketing channels, such as social media, email marketing, public relations, and advertising, to reach your audience. Craft compelling messages that highlight the unique value of your idea and encourage engagement. Monitor the response to your launch and be prepared to make adjustments based on feedback. A successful launch sets the stage for long-term success and growth.

8. Monitoring and Evaluation

After the launch, continuous monitoring and evaluation are essential to ensure ongoing success. Track key performance indicators (KPIs) to measure the effectiveness of your execution. This includes sales figures, customer feedback, and market trends. Regularly review your progress against your goals and adjust your strategies as needed.

Collect and analyse data to gain insights into what's working and what isn't. This information helps you make informed decisions and optimise your operations. Stay adaptable and open to change, as the market and customer preferences can evolve. Continuous monitoring and evaluation ensure that your idea remains relevant and successful over time.

9. Scaling and Growth

Once your idea is successfully executed, consider opportunities for scaling and growth. Scaling involves expanding your reach and increasing your impact. This could mean entering new markets, diversifying your product line, or enhancing your services. Develop a growth strategy that aligns with your long-term vision and goals.

Invest in the necessary resources and infrastructure to support growth. This may include hiring additional staff, upgrading technology, or enhancing distribution channels. Monitor the impact of your scaling efforts and adjust your strategy as needed. Sustainable growth ensures that your idea continues to thrive and achieve greater success.

10. Celebrating Success and Learning from Failure

Finally, it's important to celebrate your successes and learn from any failures along the way. Acknowledge and appreciate the hard work and achievements of yourself and your team. Celebrating success boosts morale and motivates continued effort. It also provides an opportunity to reflect on what went well and why.

Equally important is learning from failures. Every setback is a valuable learning experience that can guide future efforts. Analyse what didn't work and why, and use these insights to improve your strategies and execution. Embracing both success and failure with a growth mindset ensures continuous improvement and resilience.

The journey from idea to execution is a dynamic and rewarding process. By following these steps – generating and refining your idea, conducting research, planning and goal setting, building a team, developing a prototype, securing funding, launching and marketing, monitoring and evaluation, scaling and growth, and celebrating success and learning from failure – you can turn your ideas into reality and achieve remarkable success. Remember, every great achievement starts with a single idea, and with dedication and creativity, you can bring that idea to life.

4

How Does the Mind Function? (Left Brain Right Brain Concept)

Understanding how the mind functions is crucial for unlocking our creative potential and achieving success. One popular way to explore this is through the concept of the left brain and right brain. This theory suggests that each hemisphere of our brain is responsible for different types of thinking and tasks. While the left brain is often associated with logical and analytical thinking, the right brain is linked to creativity and intuition. In this chapter, we'll delve into the left brain-right brain concept, exploring how these two sides of our brain work together to shape our thoughts and behaviours.

The Left Brain: Logic and Analysis

The left hemisphere of the brain is often referred to as the logical side. It is responsible for tasks that involve logic, analysis, and detail-oriented thinking. This includes skills such as language, mathematics, and critical thinking. When you solve a maths problem, write an essay, or analyse data, you are primarily using your left brain. This side of the brain is structured and systematic, enabling us to process information in a linear and organised manner.

The left brain's focus on logic and structure is essential for many aspects of daily life and work. It helps us make rational decisions, understand complex concepts, and communicate effectively. For instance, when planning a project, the left brain helps break down tasks into manageable steps, set timelines, and allocate resources. By relying on logical reasoning and analytical skills, we can navigate challenges and achieve our goals efficiently.

The Right Brain: Creativity and Intuition

In contrast, the right hemisphere of the brain is often associated with creativity and intuition. This side is responsible for tasks that involve imagination, spatial awareness, and holistic thinking. When you engage in activities such as drawing, music, or brainstorming new ideas, you are primarily using your right brain. The right brain allows us to see the bigger picture, make connections between seemingly unrelated concepts, and think outside the box.

The right brain's emphasis on creativity and intuition is crucial for innovation and problem-solving. It enables us to generate novel ideas, envision new possibilities, and approach challenges from unique perspectives. For example, when designing a new product, the right brain helps us imagine how it will look, feel, and function. By tapping into our creative and intuitive abilities, we can develop innovative solutions and make significant strides in our personal and professional lives.

Balancing Both Hemispheres

While the left brain and right brain have distinct functions, they do not work in isolation. Instead, they complement each other and work together to provide a well-rounded approach to thinking and problem-solving. Achieving a balance between the two hemispheres is essential for optimal brain function and overall success. By integrating the logical and analytical skills of the left brain with the creative and intuitive abilities of the right brain, we can harness the full potential of our mind.

Balancing both hemispheres involves engaging in activities that stimulate both sides of the brain. For instance, solving puzzles, reading, and learning new languages can enhance left-brain functions, while painting, playing musical instruments, and meditation can boost right-brain functions. By incorporating a mix of these activities into our daily routine, we can develop a more balanced and versatile mind. This balance allows us to approach tasks with both precision and creativity, leading to more effective problem-solving and innovation.

The Impact on Learning and Development

Understanding the left brain-right brain concept can also have a significant impact on learning and development. Different individuals may have a dominant hemisphere, which influences their learning style and preferences. For example, left-brain dominant individuals may excel in subjects that require logical reasoning and analytical skills, such as maths and science. In contrast, right-brain dominant individuals may thrive in creative and artistic fields, such as art and music.

Recognising these differences can help tailor educational approaches to suit individual strengths and preferences. For left-brain dominant learners, structured lessons, detailed instructions, and analytical exercises can enhance their learning experience. For right-brain dominant learners, incorporating creative activities, visual aids, and open-ended projects can foster their creativity and engagement. By catering to both hemispheres, educators can create a more inclusive and effective learning environment.

Enhancing Creativity and Success

For those seeking to enhance their creativity and achieve success, understanding and leveraging the left brain-right brain concept can be highly beneficial. Engaging both hemispheres allows individuals to approach tasks with a balanced mindset, combining logical analysis with creative thinking. This integrated approach is particularly valuable in today's complex and dynamic world, where success often requires both precision and innovation.

One practical way to enhance creativity and success is by practising activities that stimulate both sides of the brain. For instance, mind mapping is a technique that encourages holistic thinking and creativity by visually organising information. Similarly, activities like journaling, where you analyse your thoughts and express your feelings, can engage both hemispheres. By regularly practising such activities, you can develop a more balanced and flexible mind, capable of tackling challenges with creativity and logic.

The Role of Mindfulness and Meditation

Mindfulness and meditation can also play a significant role in balancing the left and right brain. These practices promote mental clarity, focus, and emotional balance, which are essential for optimal brain function. Mindfulness involves being present in the moment and observing your thoughts without judgment. This practice can enhance both left-brain functions, such as attention and concentration, and right-brain functions, such as intuition and emotional awareness.

Meditation, on the other hand, can help reduce stress and enhance cognitive function. Regular meditation practice has been shown to increase the connectivity between the left and right hemispheres, promoting a more integrated and balanced brain. By incorporating mindfulness and meditation into your daily routine, you can enhance your mental well-being and unlock your creative potential. These practices provide a solid foundation for achieving success in all areas of life.

Practical Applications in the Workplace

In the workplace, understanding the left brain-right brain concept can lead to more effective teamwork and productivity. Teams that comprise individuals with diverse thinking styles can benefit from a balanced approach to problem-solving. Left-brain dominant team members can provide structure, analysis, and logical reasoning, while right-brain dominant members can contribute creativity, innovation, and holistic thinking. This diversity of thought can lead to more comprehensive and innovative solutions.

Encouraging a workplace culture that values both logical and creative thinking can also enhance overall performance. Providing opportunities for creative expression, such as brainstorming sessions, collaborative projects, and flexible workspaces, can stimulate right-brain functions. At the same time, promoting structured processes, clear communication, and analytical tools can support left-brain functions. By fostering an environment that nurtures both hemispheres, organisations can achieve greater success and innovation.

Personal Development and Self-Awareness

On a personal level, developing self-awareness about your own cognitive preferences can enhance your growth and success. Reflecting on whether you are more left-brain or right-brain dominant can help you understand your strengths and areas for improvement. This self-awareness allows you to consciously engage in activities that balance your brain functions and develop a more well-rounded mind.

For instance, if you identify as left-brain dominant, you might benefit from engaging in more creative activities to stimulate your right brain. Conversely, if you are right-brain dominant, incorporating more analytical tasks into your routine can enhance your logical thinking skills. This balanced approach to personal development can lead to greater creativity, problem-solving abilities, and overall success.

Embracing Neuroplasticity

It's important to note that the brain is highly adaptable, thanks to a phenomenon known as neuroplasticity. Neuroplasticity refers to the brain's ability to reorganise itself by forming new neural connections throughout life. This means that even if you have a dominant hemisphere, you can develop and strengthen the functions of the other hemisphere through practice and experience.

Embracing neuroplasticity involves being open to new experiences and challenges. By stepping out of your comfort zone and engaging in activities that stimulate both sides of the brain, you can enhance your cognitive flexibility and creativity. This adaptability is crucial for achieving success in a rapidly changing world. By continuously challenging your brain, you can unlock new potentials and achieve remarkable growth.

Understanding the left brain-right brain concept provides valuable insights into how our mind functions and how we can leverage this knowledge for success. By recognising the distinct roles of each hemisphere and striving for a balanced approach, we can enhance our creativity, problem-solving abilities, and overall cognitive function. Whether in learning, the workplace, or personal development, embracing both logical and creative thinking leads to a more well-rounded and successful life. Remember, your brain is a powerful tool, and by nurturing both hemispheres, you can unlock your full potential and achieve remarkable success.

5

Growth Mindset vs. Fixed Mindset

The way we perceive our abilities and approach challenges plays a crucial role in our personal and professional success. This chapter will explore the concepts of growth mindset and fixed mindset, highlighting their differences and the impact they have on our lives. By understanding these mindsets, we can unlock our potential and achieve greater success.

Understanding Growth Mindset

A growth mindset is the belief that our abilities and intelligence can be developed through dedication, effort, and learning. People with a growth mindset see challenges as opportunities to grow and view failures as valuable lessons. They believe that hard work, perseverance, and the right strategies can lead to improvement and success. This mindset fosters a love for learning and a resilience that is essential for achieving long-term goals.

For example, someone with a growth mindset might face a difficult task and think, "This is challenging, but I can learn and improve with effort." They are more likely to seek out feedback, try different approaches, and persist despite setbacks. This positive attitude towards learning and growth can lead to significant achievements and personal development.

Understanding Fixed Mindset

In contrast, a fixed mindset is the belief that our abilities and intelligence are static and unchangeable. People with a fixed mindset tend to avoid challenges, give up easily, and view effort as fruitless. They believe that talent alone leads to success, and if they fail at something, it's because they lack the inherent ability. This mindset can limit potential and hinder personal and professional growth.

For instance, someone with a fixed mindset might face the same difficult task and think, "I'm not good at this, so there's no point in trying." They might avoid seeking feedback, stick to what they know, and shy away from new experiences. This fear of failure and resistance to effort can prevent them from realising their full potential and achieving success.

The Impact on Learning and Development

The mindset we adopt significantly affects our learning and development. A growth mindset encourages continuous improvement and a love for learning. People with a growth mindset are more open to new experiences, willing to take risks, and resilient in the face of challenges. They view effort as a path to mastery and are more likely to achieve their goals over time.

In educational settings, students with a growth mindset tend to perform better academically. They are more likely to embrace challenges, seek help when needed, and persist through difficulties. This attitude not only enhances their learning experience but also prepares them for future challenges. By fostering a growth mindset, educators can help students develop a lifelong love for learning and a resilient attitude towards challenges.

The Impact on Professional Success

In the professional world, a growth mindset can be a powerful driver of success. Employees with a growth mindset are more adaptable, innovative, and committed to continuous improvement. They are more likely to take on challenging projects, seek feedback, and collaborate effectively with others. This proactive and positive attitude can lead to career advancement and personal fulfilment.

Conversely, a fixed mindset can hinder professional success. Employees with a fixed mindset may avoid challenges, fear criticism, and resist change. This can limit their growth, reduce their effectiveness, and hinder their ability to contribute to the organisation. By encouraging a growth mindset, employers can create a more dynamic, innovative, and productive work environment.

Developing a Growth Mindset

Developing a growth mindset involves changing the way we think about our abilities and approach challenges. It starts with self-awareness and recognising when we are falling into fixed mindset thinking. By challenging these thoughts and reframing them, we can cultivate a more positive and growth-oriented attitude.

One practical way to develop a growth mindset is by embracing challenges and viewing them as opportunities to learn. Instead of avoiding difficult tasks, approach them with curiosity and a willingness to learn. Seek feedback and use it to improve, rather than seeing it as a criticism of your abilities. Celebrate effort and progress, not just the final outcome. This shift in perspective can help you build resilience, enhance your learning, and achieve greater success.

Overcoming Obstacles

A growth mindset also helps us overcome obstacles and setbacks. When faced with difficulties, people with a growth mindset are more likely to persevere and find solutions. They view setbacks as part of the learning process and use them as stepping stones to future success. This resilience is crucial for achieving long-term goals and overcoming challenges.

In contrast, a fixed mindset can make obstacles seem insurmountable. People with a fixed mindset may give up easily when faced with difficulties, believing that they lack the ability to succeed. This can lead to missed opportunities and unfulfilled potential. By adopting a growth mindset, you can develop the resilience and determination needed to overcome obstacles and achieve your goals.

The Role of Effort and Perseverance

Effort and perseverance are key components of a growth mindset. People with a growth mindset understand that success requires hard work and dedication. They are willing to put in the effort to improve their skills and achieve their goals. This commitment to continuous improvement can lead to significant personal and professional achievements.

In contrast, a fixed mindset may devalue effort, seeing it as a sign of inadequacy. People with a fixed mindset may believe that if they have to work hard at something, it means they are not naturally good at it. This can discourage them from putting in the effort needed to succeed. By valuing effort and perseverance, you can develop a growth mindset and achieve greater success.

Cultivating a Growth Mindset in Others

Encouraging a growth mindset in others can have a profound impact on their success. Whether you are a parent, teacher, manager, or friend, you can help others develop a growth mindset by praising effort, encouraging learning, and supporting resilience. Focus on the process of learning and improvement, rather than just the end result.

Provide constructive feedback and celebrate progress, no matter how small. Encourage others to take on challenges, learn from failures, and keep pushing forward. By fostering a growth mindset in those around you, you can help them unlock their potential and achieve their goals.

The Long-Term Benefits

The long-term benefits of a growth mindset are significant. People with a growth mindset are more likely to achieve their goals, maintain a positive attitude, and continue growing throughout their lives. They are better equipped to handle challenges, adapt to change, and seize opportunities. This mindset not only leads to personal and professional success but also contributes to overall well-being and fulfilment.

In contrast, a fixed mindset can limit potential and hinder long-term success. People with a fixed mindset may struggle to adapt to change, miss out on opportunities, and experience lower levels of satisfaction and fulfilment. By developing and nurturing a growth mindset, you can unlock your full potential and achieve greater success and happiness in life.

Practical Tips for Developing a Growth Mindset

To develop a growth mindset, start by challenging your fixed mindset thoughts. When you catch yourself thinking, "I can't do this," reframe it to, "I can learn how to do this." Embrace challenges and view them as opportunities to grow. Celebrate effort and progress, not just the final result.

Seek out learning opportunities and be open to feedback. Surround yourself with people who have a growth mindset and can support and inspire you. Practice gratitude and focus on the positives in your journey. By consistently applying these practices, you can cultivate a growth mindset and unlock your potential for success.

The distinction between a growth mindset and a fixed mindset is profound and has a significant impact on our lives. A growth mindset fosters resilience, adaptability, and a love for learning, leading to greater personal and professional success. On the other hand, a fixed mindset can limit potential and hinder growth. By understanding and developing a growth mindset, we can unlock our potential, overcome challenges, and achieve remarkable success. Remember, your mindset is a powerful tool, and by nurturing a growth mindset, you can create a fulfilling and successful life.

6

Cultivating a Positive and Productive Mindset

A positive and productive mindset is a powerful asset in achieving success and happiness. It influences our thoughts, behaviours, and outcomes, shaping the way we approach challenges and opportunities. In this chapter, we will explore practical strategies for cultivating a mindset that fosters positivity and productivity, enabling us to thrive in all areas of life.

Understanding the Power of Mindset

Our mindset shapes our reality. A positive mindset helps us see opportunities, stay motivated, and overcome obstacles. It involves focusing on the good, maintaining an optimistic outlook, and believing in our ability to succeed. Conversely, a negative mindset can hinder progress, drain energy, and create unnecessary stress. Understanding the impact of our mindset is the first step in cultivating a positive and productive outlook.

Adopting a positive mindset doesn't mean ignoring life's challenges. Instead, it's about approaching difficulties with resilience and a can-do attitude. By recognising that our thoughts influence our emotions and actions, we can take control of our mindset and steer it towards positivity. This proactive approach enables us to navigate life's ups and downs with grace and determination.

Setting Clear and Achievable Goals

Setting clear and achievable goals is a fundamental aspect of a productive mindset. Goals give us direction, purpose, and a sense of accomplishment. To be effective, goals should be specific, measurable, achievable, relevant, and time-bound (SMART). By setting SMART goals, we can create a roadmap for success and stay focused on our priorities.

Breaking down larger goals into smaller, manageable tasks can make them less daunting and more attainable. Each small step completed brings us closer to our ultimate objective, boosting our confidence and motivation. This structured approach helps maintain momentum and prevents overwhelm, making the journey towards our goals more manageable and enjoyable.

Practising Gratitude

Gratitude is a powerful tool for cultivating a positive mindset. By regularly acknowledging and appreciating the good in our lives, we can shift our focus away from negative thoughts and feelings. Practising gratitude can be as simple as writing down three things you're grateful for each day or expressing thanks to someone who has positively impacted your life.

Gratitude helps reframe our perspective, highlighting the positive aspects of our experiences. This shift can improve our mood, enhance our relationships, and increase overall happiness. By making gratitude a daily habit, we can create a more positive and uplifting mindset that supports our well-being and success.

Embracing Positive Self-Talk

The way we talk to ourselves greatly affects our mindset. Positive self-talk involves replacing negative, self-defeating thoughts with encouraging and empowering ones. Instead of focusing on what you can't do, remind yourself of your strengths and capabilities. Affirmations, such as "I am capable," "I can overcome this," and "I am worthy of success," can help reinforce a positive self-image.

Negative self-talk can create self-doubt and limit our potential. By consciously practising positive self-talk, we can build confidence and resilience. This positive internal dialogue helps us stay motivated, overcome setbacks, and maintain a productive mindset even in challenging situations.

Managing Stress Effectively

Stress is a common barrier to a positive and productive mindset. Learning to manage stress effectively is crucial for maintaining mental clarity and focus. Techniques such as mindfulness, meditation, deep breathing, and regular exercise can help reduce stress levels and improve overall well-being.

Mindfulness and meditation involve paying attention to the present moment without judgment. These practices can help calm the mind, reduce anxiety, and improve concentration. Regular physical activity, such as walking, yoga, or sports, also helps release tension and boost mood. By incorporating stress management techniques into our daily routine, we can create a more balanced and positive mindset.

Developing Resilience

Resilience is the ability to bounce back from setbacks and persevere through difficulties. Cultivating resilience involves adopting a growth mindset, viewing challenges as opportunities for growth, and maintaining a positive outlook. Resilient individuals are more likely to stay focused and motivated, even in the face of adversity.

Building resilience requires self-awareness and the ability to adapt to changing circumstances. Practising self-care, seeking support from others, and learning from past experiences can strengthen our resilience. By developing this crucial trait, we can navigate life's challenges with confidence and maintain a productive mindset.

Creating a Supportive Environment

Our environment plays a significant role in shaping our mindset. Surrounding ourselves with positive, supportive people can enhance our mood and motivation. Seek out relationships that inspire and uplift you, and minimise interactions with individuals who drain your energy or foster negativity.

In addition to social support, creating a physical environment that promotes positivity and productivity is essential. This might involve decluttering your workspace, adding inspirational quotes or artwork, and ensuring you have a comfortable and organised area to focus on your tasks. A supportive environment can help maintain a positive mindset and enhance overall productivity.

Continuous Learning and Growth

A commitment to continuous learning and growth is key to maintaining a productive mindset. Embrace opportunities to acquire new skills, expand your knowledge, and challenge yourself. Whether through formal education, reading, workshops, or online courses, continuous learning keeps your mind engaged and adaptable.

A growth mindset, which embraces learning and improvement, helps us stay motivated and open to new possibilities. By seeking out new challenges and viewing them as opportunities for growth, we can maintain a positive and productive attitude. This commitment to personal and professional development fuels our success and enhances our overall well-being.

Celebrating Successes and Milestones

Celebrating successes and milestones, no matter how small, reinforces a positive mindset and boosts motivation. Take time to acknowledge and appreciate your achievements, and share your successes with others. Celebrating milestones provides a sense of accomplishment and encourages continued effort towards your goals.

Reflecting on your progress and recognising your hard work helps build confidence and resilience. It's important to celebrate not only the big wins but also the small steps that contribute to your overall success. This practice of acknowledging and celebrating achievements fosters a positive and productive mindset, inspiring further growth and development.

Practising Self-Compassion

Self-compassion involves treating yourself with kindness and understanding, especially during difficult times. It's about recognising that everyone makes mistakes and experiences setbacks, and it's okay to be imperfect. Practising self-compassion helps reduce self-criticism and fosters a more positive and forgiving attitude towards oneself.

When faced with challenges or failures, instead of harshly judging yourself, offer yourself the same kindness and support you would give a friend. This compassionate approach helps maintain a positive mindset and promotes emotional well-being. By practising self-compassion, you can build resilience and stay motivated, even when things don't go as planned.

Cultivating a positive and productive mindset is a transformative journey that can significantly enhance your personal and professional life. By understanding the power of mindset, setting clear goals, practising gratitude, embracing positive self-talk, managing stress, developing resilience, creating a supportive environment, committing to continuous learning, celebrating successes, and practising self-compassion, you can create a mindset that supports your success and well-being. Remember, your mindset is a powerful tool, and by nurturing it, you can unlock your full potential and achieve remarkable success.

7

Creativity: Definition, Myths and Misconceptions

Creativity is a powerful and essential skill that influences every aspect of our lives. It fuels innovation, problem-solving, and personal fulfilment. However, creativity is often misunderstood, surrounded by myths and misconceptions that can hinder our ability to fully embrace and develop this valuable trait. In this chapter, we will define creativity, explore its importance, and debunk common myths and misconceptions, helping you to unlock your creative potential.

Defining Creativity

Creativity is the ability to generate new, original, and valuable ideas. It involves seeing the world in new ways, finding hidden patterns, and making connections between seemingly unrelated phenomena. Creativity is not limited to artistic pursuits; it encompasses all areas of life, from science and business to everyday problem-solving. At its core, creativity is about thinking outside the box and approaching challenges with an open and imaginative mind.

Creativity can manifest in various forms, such as developing innovative products, finding unique solutions to problems, or expressing oneself through art and literature. It is a dynamic process that requires both divergent thinking, which involves generating multiple ideas, and convergent thinking, which involves refining and evaluating those ideas. By understanding and embracing the multifaceted nature of creativity, we can tap into our potential and achieve greater success and satisfaction in our personal and professional lives.

The Importance of Creativity

Creativity is essential for progress and innovation. It drives advancements in technology, science, and medicine, leading to new discoveries and solutions that improve our lives. In the business world, creativity is a key factor in developing unique products and services that set companies apart from their competitors. Creative thinking also enhances problem-solving skills, enabling individuals and organisations to navigate challenges and seize opportunities effectively.

Moreover, creativity contributes to personal growth and well-being. Engaging in creative activities can boost mental health, reduce stress, and increase overall happiness. It provides an outlet for self-expression and helps individuals connect with their inner selves. By nurturing creativity, we can lead more fulfilling and balanced lives, continuously learning and growing in the process.

Myth 1: Creativity is an Inborn Talent

One of the most pervasive myths about creativity is that it is an inborn talent possessed only by a select few. This misconception suggests that you either have creativity or you don't, implying that it cannot be developed or nurtured. In reality, creativity is a skill that can be cultivated and improved over time. While some people may have a natural inclination towards creative thinking, everyone has the potential to develop their creative abilities with practice and effort.

Just like any other skill, creativity can be honed through education, experience, and dedication. Engaging in creative activities, seeking out new experiences, and challenging yourself to think differently can enhance your creative thinking skills. By adopting a growth mindset and believing in your ability to improve, you can unlock your creative potential and achieve remarkable results.

Myth 2: Creativity is Only for Artists

Another common misconception is that creativity is limited to the arts, such as painting, writing, or music. While these are certainly creative pursuits, creativity is not confined to artistic endeavours. It is a valuable skill in all fields, including science, technology, business, and education. Creative thinking is essential for developing innovative solutions, improving processes, and driving progress in any area of life.

For example, a scientist may use creative thinking to develop a new hypothesis, a business leader may innovate a new marketing strategy, and a teacher may design engaging lesson plans. Creativity is about thinking in new and original ways, regardless of the context. By recognising the broad applications of creativity, we can appreciate its importance and strive to incorporate it into all aspects of our lives.

Myth 3: Creativity Comes from the Lone Genius

The image of the lone genius, working in isolation and coming up with groundbreaking ideas, is a romantic but misleading notion. While individual creativity is important, collaboration and teamwork often play a crucial role in the creative process. Many of the greatest innovations and discoveries have resulted from collaborative efforts, where diverse perspectives and skills come together to create something new.

Collaboration fosters creativity by allowing individuals to share ideas, build on each other's strengths, and challenge each other's assumptions. Working with others can lead to more innovative and well-rounded solutions than working alone. By embracing collaboration and valuing the contributions of others, we can enhance our creative potential and achieve greater success.

Myth 4: Creativity is Spontaneous and Uncontrollable

Many people believe that creativity is a spontaneous and uncontrollable burst of inspiration that cannot be summoned at will. While moments of sudden insight do occur, creativity is also a disciplined process that involves deliberate practice and effort. Creative individuals often follow structured routines, engage in regular practice, and use specific techniques to stimulate their creativity.

Setting aside dedicated time for creative activities, using brainstorming techniques, and creating an environment that fosters creativity can help generate new ideas and solutions. By recognising that creativity is a skill that can be developed through intentional practice, we can take proactive steps to enhance our creative thinking and achieve our goals.

Myth 5: Creativity Requires Total Freedom

The idea that creativity requires total freedom and lack of constraints is another common misconception. While some degree of freedom is important, constraints can actually enhance creativity by providing structure and focus. Limitations can challenge us to think more creatively and find innovative solutions within the given parameters.

For example, a writer might find inspiration in the challenge of writing a story within a specific word count, or a designer might come up with a unique solution when faced with budget constraints. Embracing constraints as opportunities rather than obstacles can lead to more creative and effective outcomes. By understanding the role of constraints in the creative process, we can leverage them to our advantage and enhance our creativity.

Myth 6: Creativity is Effortless

The notion that creativity is effortless and comes naturally to those who are "gifted" is another myth that can discourage people from pursuing creative endeavours. In reality, creativity often involves hard work, perseverance, and a willingness to face failure. Creative individuals put in significant effort to develop their skills, experiment with new ideas, and refine their work.

Thomas Edison's famous quote, "Genius is one percent inspiration and ninety-nine percent perspiration," highlights the importance of effort in the creative process. By recognising that creativity requires dedication and persistence, we can approach our creative pursuits with the right mindset and work ethic. This understanding empowers us to keep pushing forward, even when faced with challenges and setbacks.

Debunking Myths to Unlock Creativity

Understanding and debunking these myths and misconceptions about creativity is essential for unlocking our creative potential. By recognising that creativity is a skill that can be developed, embracing collaboration and constraints, and appreciating the effort involved, we can cultivate a more realistic and empowering view of creativity.

Adopting a growth mindset, seeking out new experiences, and practising creative thinking techniques can help us enhance our creativity. By challenging these myths and embracing a more inclusive and dynamic understanding of creativity, we can unlock our potential and achieve greater success and fulfilment in our personal and professional lives.

Practical Tips for Cultivating Creativity

To cultivate creativity, consider incorporating the following practices into your routine:

1. **Set Aside Time for Creative Activities**: Dedicate regular time for creative pursuits, whether it's brainstorming, writing, drawing, or experimenting with new ideas.
2. **Embrace New Experiences**: Seek out new experiences and challenges that push you out of your comfort zone and stimulate your imagination.
3. **Collaborate with Others**: Engage in collaborative projects and share ideas with others to benefit from diverse perspectives and insights.
4. **Use Creative Thinking Techniques**: Practice techniques such as mind mapping, brainstorming, and lateral thinking to generate new ideas and solutions.
5. **Create a Stimulating Environment**: Surround yourself with inspiring materials, such as books, art, and music, to spark your creativity.
6. **Reflect and Learn from Failures**: View failures as opportunities to learn and grow, and use them to refine your creative process.

By incorporating these practices into your daily life, you can cultivate a more creative mindset and unlock your potential for innovation and success.

Creativity is a powerful and essential skill that can be cultivated and developed. By understanding its true nature and debunking common myths and misconceptions, we can unlock our creative potential and achieve greater success and fulfilment. Remember, creativity is not limited to a select few or specific fields; it is a dynamic process that involves thinking differently and embracing new possibilities. By nurturing our creativity and approaching challenges with an open and imaginative mind, we can achieve remarkable results in all areas of life.

8

The Science Behind Creative Thinking

Creative thinking is a fascinating and complex process that plays a crucial role in innovation and problem-solving. While creativity often seems mysterious and spontaneous, scientific research helps us understand how it works. In this chapter, we will explore the science behind creative thinking, examining the brain processes, psychological factors, and environmental influences that contribute to our ability to generate new and innovative ideas.

Understanding Brain Function and Creativity

Creativity involves multiple areas of the brain working together in complex ways. Traditionally, creativity was associated primarily with the right hemisphere of the brain, known for its role in artistic and spatial tasks. However, recent research has shown that creativity involves both hemispheres. The left hemisphere, responsible for logical and analytical thinking, also plays a crucial role in the creative process. This collaboration between the two sides of the brain enables us to combine logical analysis with imaginative thinking.

Neuroscientists have identified specific brain networks that are active during creative thinking. The default mode network

(DMN) is one of these networks and is associated with spontaneous thinking, daydreaming, and imagination. The executive control network (ECN), on the other hand, is involved in focused attention and problem-solving. The interplay between these networks allows the brain to generate creative ideas by combining spontaneous thoughts with controlled, goal-directed processes.

The Role of Neurotransmitters

Neurotransmitters are chemicals in the brain that transmit signals between neurons. They play a crucial role in regulating mood, cognition, and behaviour, and they also influence creativity. Dopamine, often referred to as the "feel-good" neurotransmitter, is particularly important in the creative process. It is associated with reward and motivation, and higher levels of dopamine can enhance creative thinking by increasing our ability to explore new ideas and take risks.

Serotonin and norepinephrine are other neurotransmitters that affect creativity. Serotonin helps regulate mood and emotional balance, which can impact our ability to think creatively. Norepinephrine, involved in attention and arousal, can enhance our focus and drive during creative tasks. Understanding the role of these neurotransmitters can help us create conditions that foster creativity, such as maintaining a positive mood and staying motivated.

The Importance of Divergent and Convergent Thinking

Creative thinking involves two key processes: divergent thinking and convergent thinking. Divergent thinking is the ability to generate many different ideas or solutions to a problem. It involves brainstorming, free association, and exploring multiple possibilities without immediate judgment. Divergent thinking is crucial for the initial stages of the creative process, as it allows for the exploration of a wide range of ideas.

Convergent thinking, on the other hand, involves evaluating and refining ideas to arrive at the best solution. It requires logical analysis, critical thinking, and decision-making. Convergent thinking is essential for narrowing down options and implementing creative ideas effectively. The balance between divergent and convergent thinking enables us to not only generate innovative ideas but also to refine and execute them successfully.

The Influence of Personality Traits

Certain personality traits are associated with higher levels of creativity. Openness to experience, one of the five major personality traits, is strongly linked to creative thinking. Individuals who score high in openness tend to be curious, imaginative, and willing to explore new ideas. This openness allows them to consider unconventional solutions and think outside the box.

Other traits that influence creativity include intrinsic motivation, resilience, and a willingness to take risks. Intrinsic motivation, the drive to engage in an activity for its own sake, enhances creativity by fostering a deep interest and enjoyment in the creative process. Resilience helps individuals persist through challenges and setbacks, while a willingness to take risks encourages them to explore uncharted territories and experiment with novel ideas. Cultivating these traits can enhance our creative potential and lead to greater innovation and success.

The Role of Environment and Context

The environment and context in which we find ourselves can significantly impact our creative thinking. A stimulating and supportive environment can enhance creativity by providing inspiration and resources. Factors such as physical space, social interactions, and cultural influences play a crucial role in shaping our creative abilities. For example, a cluttered and chaotic workspace may hinder creativity, while an organised and aesthetically pleasing environment can foster it.

Social interactions and collaborations also contribute to creativity. Engaging with diverse perspectives and ideas can lead to new insights and innovative solutions. Brainstorming sessions, group discussions, and collaborative projects create opportunities for creative thinking to flourish. Additionally, cultural influences, such as exposure to different art forms, traditions, and ways of thinking, can broaden our creative horizons and inspire new ideas.

The Impact of Sleep and Relaxation

Sleep and relaxation are essential for creative thinking. Research has shown that adequate sleep improves cognitive function, including creativity. During sleep, the brain processes and consolidates information, making connections between seemingly unrelated ideas. This process, known as incubation, can lead to creative insights and problem-solving. Ensuring sufficient rest and relaxation can enhance our ability to think creatively and generate innovative solutions.

Relaxation techniques, such as mindfulness and meditation, also play a role in fostering creativity. These practices help reduce stress and improve focus, allowing the mind to wander and explore new possibilities. When we are relaxed, our brain is more likely to make unique connections and generate novel ideas. Incorporating regular relaxation practices into our routine can create a mental environment conducive to creative thinking.

The Power of Incubation and Breaks

Incubation is a critical phase in the creative process where ideas are given time to percolate. This phase often occurs during periods of rest or distraction, allowing the subconscious mind to work on problems without deliberate effort. Taking breaks and stepping away from a problem can lead to sudden insights and breakthroughs. This phenomenon, often referred to as the "aha moment," is when a solution or creative idea suddenly becomes clear.

Breaks and downtime are not just about rest; they provide essential opportunities for the brain to synthesise information and form new connections. Engaging in activities that are enjoyable and unrelated to the task at hand, such as taking a walk, listening to music, or even daydreaming, can facilitate this incubation process. By intentionally incorporating breaks and periods of relaxation, we can enhance our creative capabilities.

The Role of Failure and Risk-Taking

Embracing failure and taking risks are integral parts of the creative process. Fear of failure can stifle creativity and prevent us from exploring new ideas. However, viewing failure as a learning opportunity allows us to experiment and innovate without the fear of negative consequences. Creative individuals often experience numerous failures before achieving success, as each failure provides valuable insights and fosters growth.

Risk-taking is also essential for creativity. It involves stepping outside of our comfort zones and trying new approaches. This willingness to take risks can lead to unexpected and innovative outcomes. By cultivating a mindset that embraces failure and encourages risk-taking, we can create an environment where creativity thrives.

Enhancing Creativity Through Practice

Like any other skill, creativity can be enhanced through deliberate practice. Engaging in creative exercises, such as brainstorming sessions, free writing, or drawing, can strengthen our creative muscles. These activities encourage divergent thinking and help develop our ability to generate and refine ideas. Setting aside time for regular creative practice can lead to significant improvements in our creative thinking abilities.

Additionally, seeking out new experiences and learning opportunities can fuel creativity. Exposing ourselves to different cultures, fields of study, and hobbies broadens our knowledge base and provides fresh perspectives. This diversity of experiences can spark new ideas and enhance our ability to think creatively. By continuously challenging ourselves and seeking growth, we can keep our creative abilities sharp and dynamic.

Leveraging Technology for Creativity

Technology can be a powerful tool for enhancing creativity. Digital tools and platforms provide new ways to generate, organise, and share ideas. For example, mind-mapping software, collaborative platforms, and design tools can facilitate the creative process by making it easier to visualise and develop concepts. Additionally, access to vast amounts of information and resources online can inspire and inform our creative endeavours.

However, it's important to strike a balance and avoid over-reliance on technology. While digital tools can enhance creativity, excessive use of technology can lead to distractions and reduce our ability to think deeply. Setting boundaries and using technology mindfully can help us leverage its benefits while maintaining focus and fostering our creative thinking.

Cultivating a Creative Mindset

Ultimately, cultivating a creative mindset involves adopting attitudes and behaviours that support creative thinking. This includes being open to new ideas, embracing curiosity, and maintaining a willingness to experiment and take risks. Developing resilience and a positive attitude towards failure is also crucial, as it allows us to learn and grow from our experiences.

Nurturing a sense of playfulness and wonder can also enhance creativity. Approaching tasks with a playful attitude encourages experimentation and reduces the pressure to produce perfect results. By fostering a mindset that values curiosity, exploration, and continuous learning, we can create an environment where creativity flourishes.

Understanding the science behind creative thinking provides valuable insights into how we can cultivate and enhance our creative abilities. By exploring the roles of brain function, neurotransmitters, personality traits, and environmental influences, we can develop strategies to foster creativity in our personal and professional lives. Embracing practices such as relaxation, incubation, risk-taking, and deliberate practice can further enhance our creative potential. Ultimately, cultivating a creative mindset involves adopting attitudes and behaviours that support and nurture our natural capacity for innovation and imaginative thinking. By doing so, we can unlock our full creative potential and achieve greater success and fulfilment.

9

The Power of Creative Collaboration

Creative collaboration is a powerful force that drives innovation, solves complex problems, and brings out the best in individuals. When people come together to share ideas, knowledge, and skills, the collective creativity can produce remarkable results. In this chapter, we will explore the benefits of creative collaboration, how to foster a collaborative environment, and the impact it can have on personal and professional success.

The Benefits of Creative Collaboration

Creative collaboration combines diverse perspectives and expertise, leading to richer and more innovative ideas. When people with different backgrounds and skills work together, they bring unique viewpoints that can challenge conventional thinking and inspire new solutions. This diversity of thought is one of the key strengths of collaborative creativity, as it allows for the synthesis of varied ideas into something truly novel.

Moreover, collaboration fosters a sense of shared purpose and motivation. Working with others towards a common goal can enhance individual commitment and drive. Team members support and inspire each other, creating a positive feedback loop that boosts morale and productivity. This collective effort often leads to outcomes that exceed what individuals could achieve on their own.

Enhancing Problem-Solving Capabilities

Collaborative creativity is particularly effective in problem-solving. Complex problems often require multifaceted solutions that can benefit from multiple perspectives. When a team works together, they can break down a problem into smaller parts and tackle each aspect with specialised knowledge. This collective approach can uncover insights and solutions that might be missed by an individual working alone.

Furthermore, collaboration encourages critical thinking and constructive feedback. Team members can challenge each other's assumptions, question ideas, and refine solutions through discussion and debate. This iterative process of feedback and improvement can lead to more robust and effective solutions, demonstrating the power of collaborative problem-solving.

Building Stronger Relationships

Creative collaboration also strengthens relationships and builds a sense of community. Working closely with others fosters trust, respect, and mutual understanding. These strong interpersonal connections are valuable in both personal and professional contexts, as they create a supportive network that can provide assistance and encouragement.

In a professional setting, collaborative projects can enhance team cohesion and cooperation. When colleagues work together creatively, they develop a deeper appreciation for each other's skills and contributions. This positive dynamic can lead to a more harmonious and productive work environment, where collaboration becomes a natural and integral part of the organisational culture.

Leveraging Individual Strengths

One of the significant advantages of creative collaboration is the ability to leverage individual strengths. Each team member brings unique talents, experiences, and knowledge to the table. By recognising and utilising these strengths, a team can maximise its overall effectiveness and creativity. For example, one person might excel in generating innovative ideas, while another is skilled in executing plans and managing details.

This complementary dynamic allows for a more efficient division of labour, where tasks are assigned based on individual strengths and expertise. By doing so, the team can operate more smoothly and achieve higher-quality results. Leveraging individual strengths through collaboration not only enhances the final outcome but also promotes personal growth and job satisfaction.

Fostering a Collaborative Environment

Creating an environment that encourages creative collaboration is essential for harnessing its full potential. This involves promoting open communication, mutual respect, and a willingness to share ideas. Leaders play a crucial role in fostering such an environment by setting the tone and providing the necessary resources and support.

Encouraging open dialogue and brainstorming sessions can stimulate creative thinking and idea sharing. Providing opportunities for team-building activities and collaborative projects can also strengthen bonds and improve teamwork. Additionally, recognising and celebrating collaborative achievements can reinforce the value of teamwork and motivate individuals to continue working together creatively.

Overcoming Challenges in Collaboration

While creative collaboration has many benefits, it can also present challenges. Differences in opinions, communication styles, and working methods can sometimes lead to conflicts and misunderstandings. However, these challenges can be overcome with effective communication and conflict resolution strategies.

Encouraging active listening and empathy can help team members understand each other's perspectives and work through disagreements constructively. Establishing clear goals, roles, and expectations can also reduce potential conflicts and ensure that everyone is aligned and working towards the same objectives. By addressing challenges proactively, teams can maintain a positive and productive collaborative environment.

The Role of Technology in Collaboration

Technology plays a significant role in facilitating creative collaboration, especially in today's digital age. Online collaboration tools, such as project management software, communication platforms, and shared digital workspaces, enable teams to work together seamlessly, regardless of geographical location. These tools provide a centralised platform for sharing ideas, tracking progress, and communicating in real time.

Virtual collaboration tools can also enhance creativity by providing new ways to brainstorm and visualise ideas. For example, digital whiteboards and mind-mapping tools allow team members to contribute and organise their thoughts collaboratively. By leveraging technology, teams can overcome physical barriers and work together more effectively, tapping into a global pool of ideas and talents.

The Impact on Personal Growth

Engaging in creative collaboration can have a profound impact on personal growth and development. Working with others exposes individuals to new ideas, perspectives, and skills. This exposure can broaden their horizons, enhance their knowledge, and inspire them to think more creatively. Collaborative experiences also help individuals develop important soft skills, such as communication, teamwork, and problem-solving.

Moreover, being part of a successful collaborative effort can boost confidence and self-esteem. The sense of accomplishment that comes from achieving a common goal with others reinforces the value of teamwork and encourages individuals to seek out more collaborative opportunities. This continuous learning and growth contribute to long-term personal and professional success.

Case Studies of Successful Collaboration

There are numerous examples of successful creative collaboration across different fields. In the world of business, companies like Apple and Google have thrived by fostering a collaborative culture that encourages innovation and teamwork. Their success demonstrates how creative collaboration can drive industry-leading innovations and maintain a competitive edge.

In the arts, collaborations between artists, musicians, and writers often lead to groundbreaking works that push the boundaries of their respective fields. These creative partnerships showcase how combining diverse talents and perspectives can result in extraordinary achievements. Studying these case studies can provide valuable insights into the principles and practices that make creative collaboration successful.

Cultivating a Collaborative Mindset

To fully harness the power of creative collaboration, it is essential to cultivate a collaborative mindset. This involves being open to new ideas, willing to share knowledge, and ready to work with others towards common goals. Developing this mindset requires self-awareness, adaptability, and a commitment to continuous learning.

Individuals can cultivate a collaborative mindset by seeking out opportunities to collaborate, actively participating in team activities, and reflecting on their experiences. Embracing a growth mindset, where challenges are seen as opportunities for learning, can also enhance one's ability to collaborate effectively. By adopting a collaborative mindset, individuals can contribute more meaningfully to their teams and achieve greater success.

The power of creative collaboration lies in its ability to combine diverse perspectives, leverage individual strengths, and foster innovation. By understanding and embracing the benefits of collaboration, we can create environments that support and encourage teamwork. Overcoming challenges, leveraging technology, and cultivating a collaborative mindset are essential steps in harnessing the full potential of creative collaboration. Through collaboration, we can achieve remarkable outcomes and drive success in our personal and professional lives.

10

Building a Network of Like-Minded Individuals

Building a network of like-minded individuals is a powerful strategy for personal and professional growth. A strong network provides support, inspiration, and opportunities that can help you achieve your goals. In this chapter, we will explore the benefits of building such a network, practical steps to create and maintain it, and how to leverage your network for success.

The Benefits of a Like-Minded Network

Having a network of like-minded individuals offers numerous benefits. Firstly, it provides a support system that can offer advice, encouragement, and understanding. Whether you're facing challenges or celebrating successes, having people who share your interests and values can make a significant difference in your journey. They can offer insights and perspectives that you might not have considered, helping you navigate through difficulties and make informed decisions.

Moreover, a like-minded network fosters collaboration and innovation. When people with similar goals and interests come together, they can brainstorm new ideas, collaborate on projects, and create innovative solutions. This synergy can lead to exciting opportunities and developments that might not have been possible working alone. Sharing knowledge and resources within your network can accelerate progress and lead to mutual success.

Identifying Like-Minded Individuals

The first step in building a network of like-minded individuals is identifying people who share your interests, values, and goals. Start by considering your own passions and objectives. What are your core interests? What values are important to you? What are your long-term goals? Understanding your own identity will help you recognise like-minded individuals who align with your vision.

Look for people in your existing circles who share similar interests. This could be colleagues, friends, or acquaintances. Attend events, workshops, and conferences related to your interests. These gatherings are excellent opportunities to meet people with shared passions. Online platforms, such as social media groups, forums, and professional networks like LinkedIn, are also valuable resources for connecting with like-minded individuals from around the world.

Building Genuine Connections

Building a network of like-minded individuals is not just about collecting contacts; it's about establishing genuine connections. Take the time to get to know the people you meet. Engage in meaningful conversations, ask questions, and show genuine interest in their experiences and perspectives. Building trust and rapport is essential for creating strong and lasting relationships.

Be authentic and open in your interactions. Share your own experiences, goals, and challenges. Authenticity fosters trust and encourages others to open up as well. Remember that relationships are a two-way street; offer your support and assistance whenever possible. By being a valuable and reliable member of your network, you can build strong, mutually beneficial connections.

Leveraging Technology to Connect

In today's digital age, technology provides powerful tools for building and maintaining a network of like-minded individuals. Social media platforms, professional networking sites, and online communities make it easier than ever to connect with people who share your interests. Use these tools to reach out, join groups, participate in discussions, and share your own insights.

Virtual events and webinars are also great opportunities to connect with like-minded individuals. These events often include networking sessions where you can meet people from various locations. Use video conferencing tools to have face-to-face conversations and build deeper connections. By leveraging technology effectively, you can expand your network beyond geographical limitations and connect with a diverse group of like-minded individuals.

Participating in Communities and Groups

Joining communities and groups related to your interests is a great way to meet like-minded individuals. Look for local clubs, organisations, or online communities where people with similar passions gather. These groups provide a platform for networking, collaboration, and mutual support. Actively participate in these communities by attending meetings, contributing to discussions, and volunteering for activities.

Participation in these groups not only helps you build connections but also enhances your skills and knowledge. Engaging with others who share your interests can provide new insights, ideas, and opportunities for growth. By being an active and contributing member of these communities, you can establish yourself as a valuable and respected participant, further strengthening your network.

Attending Networking Events

Networking events, such as conferences, seminars, and workshops, offer excellent opportunities to meet like-minded individuals. These events bring together people with shared interests and goals, creating a conducive environment for networking. Prepare for these events by setting clear objectives, such as meeting specific individuals, learning about certain topics, or finding potential collaborators.

During networking events, approach people with confidence and genuine interest. Start conversations by asking about their work, interests, and goals. Exchange contact information and follow up with personalised messages after the event. Building a network through events requires proactive engagement and follow-up, but the connections made can be incredibly valuable for your personal and professional growth.

Maintaining and Nurturing Your Network

Building a network is just the beginning; maintaining and nurturing it is equally important. Stay in touch with the people in your network through regular communication. This could be through emails, social media interactions, or occasional phone calls. Share updates about your own progress and achievements, and show interest in their developments as well.

Offer your support and assistance whenever possible. Whether it's providing advice, sharing resources, or helping with a project, being a helpful and reliable contact strengthens your relationships. Attend reunions, catch-up sessions, or organise informal meet-ups to maintain personal connections. By nurturing your network, you can ensure that your relationships remain strong and beneficial over time.

Offering Value to Your Network

To build a successful network of like-minded individuals, it's essential to offer value to your connections. Think about how you can contribute to their success and well-being. This could be through sharing knowledge, providing support, or connecting them with other valuable contacts. Offering value builds trust and reciprocity, making your network more robust and supportive.

Consider creating and sharing content that benefits your network. This could be blog posts, articles, or resources related to your shared interests. Hosting events, webinars, or discussion groups can also provide value and strengthen your connections. By consistently offering value, you position yourself as a valuable and respected member of your network, enhancing the mutual benefits of your relationships.

Leveraging Your Network for Opportunities

Once you've built a strong network of like-minded individuals, you can leverage it for various opportunities. Whether you're looking for career advancements, business collaborations, or personal development, your network can be a valuable resource. Reach out to your contacts for advice, introductions, or collaboration opportunities. Don't hesitate to ask for help when needed, as a strong network is built on mutual support and cooperation.

When leveraging your network, always approach with respect and consideration. Make sure your requests are reasonable and beneficial to both parties. Express gratitude for any assistance provided and reciprocate when possible. By leveraging your network thoughtfully and respectfully, you can unlock numerous opportunities for growth and success.

Learning and Growing Together

A network of like-minded individuals is not just about achieving individual goals; it's also about learning and growing together. Engage in continuous learning and development with your network by sharing resources, attending workshops, and participating in discussions. Collaborate on projects and initiatives that align with your shared interests and goals.

By learning and growing together, you can inspire and motivate each other to reach new heights. The collective knowledge, skills, and experiences within your network can provide a wealth of opportunities for personal and professional development. Embrace the journey of growth and success together, and celebrate each other's achievements along the way.

Building a network of like-minded individuals is a powerful strategy for achieving success and fulfilment. By identifying and connecting with people who share your interests and values, you can create a supportive and inspiring community. Leveraging technology, participating in communities and events, and offering value to your connections are key steps in building and maintaining a strong network. By nurturing these relationships and leveraging your network for opportunities, you can unlock your full potential and achieve remarkable success. Remember, the power of a like-minded network lies in the mutual support, collaboration, and growth that it fosters. Embrace this journey and build a network that empowers you to reach your goals and aspirations.

11

Measure Creativity

Creativity is an essential skill that fuels innovation, problem-solving, and personal expression. But how can you measure something as abstract and dynamic as creativity? While it may seem challenging, there are several methods and tools available to assess your creative potential. In this chapter, we'll explore various ways to measure creativity, helping you understand your strengths and identify areas for growth.

Understanding Creativity

Before diving into measurement, it's important to understand what creativity entails. Creativity involves generating new and valuable ideas by thinking outside the box and making unique connections. It's not confined to the arts; creativity is equally vital in science, business, technology, and everyday life. Everyone has the potential to be creative, but recognising and nurturing this trait is key to unlocking it fully.

Creativity can manifest in numerous ways, from artistic expression and innovative problem-solving to inventive product design and novel approaches to everyday tasks. A scientist developing a new theory, a chef creating an original recipe, or an entrepreneur launching a groundbreaking business all exhibit creativity. Understanding this broad spectrum allows us to appreciate the various forms creativity can take and sets the stage for measuring it effectively.

Self-Assessment Tools

One of the most accessible ways to measure creativity is through self-assessment tools and questionnaires. These tools evaluate different aspects of creative thinking, such as originality, flexibility, and problem-solving skills. The Torrance Tests of Creative Thinking (TTCT) is a well-known example, designed to assess divergent thinking – the ability to generate multiple solutions to a problem.

Self-assessment tools typically involve tasks or questions that reveal your creative thinking patterns. For example, you might be asked to come up with as many uses as possible for a common object, solve hypothetical problems creatively, or complete unfinished drawings. These tasks help identify your creative strengths and areas for improvement, providing a baseline from which you can develop further.

Observing Your Creative Process

Another effective method to measure creativity is by observing your creative process. Pay attention to how you approach tasks and challenges. Do you brainstorm extensively? Are you open to experimenting with different methods? Do you persist in finding innovative solutions despite obstacles? Documenting these behaviours can offer valuable insights into your creative mindset.

Maintaining a creativity journal is an excellent way to track your creative process. Record your ideas, the steps you take to develop them, and your reflections on creative tasks. Note patterns in your thinking, such as how you generate ideas, refine them, and overcome difficulties. This self-reflection can help you identify strengths and areas for growth, enabling you to enhance your creative abilities consciously.

Seeking Feedback from Others

Feedback from others can provide a different perspective on your creativity. Friends, colleagues, or mentors might notice strengths and talents that you overlook. Constructive feedback can offer valuable insights into how others perceive your creative abilities and provide suggestions for improvement.

Engaging in collaborative projects or creative communities can be particularly beneficial. Working with others allows you to compare your creative approaches and gain new ideas. It also provides opportunities for receiving feedback in a supportive environment. This external perspective can help validate your self-assessment and reveal aspects of your creativity that you might not be aware of.

Creative Achievement Questionnaires

Creative achievement questionnaires are another method to measure creativity. These tools assess your creative accomplishments across various domains, such as arts, science, and entrepreneurship. The Creative Achievement Questionnaire (CAQ) is a popular example, asking you to list your achievements in different fields and rate their significance.

Completing such questionnaires helps you take stock of your creative milestones and recognise your contributions. It provides a tangible record of your creative journey, highlighting areas where you have excelled and identifying domains that might benefit from further exploration. Reflecting on your achievements can boost your confidence and motivate you to pursue new creative challenges.

Performance-Based Assessments

Performance-based assessments involve completing tasks or projects that require creative thinking. These assessments evaluate your ability to generate ideas, solve problems, and produce original work. Examples include writing essays, designing products, creating artworks, or developing innovative solutions to real-world issues.

Performance-based assessments provide a practical measure of creativity by focusing on actual output rather than self-reported abilities. They allow for a comprehensive evaluation of your creative skills, including idea generation, execution, and refinement. By reviewing the results of these assessments, you can gain insights into your creative strengths and identify areas for further development.

Brainstorming Sessions

Brainstorming sessions are a dynamic way to measure and enhance creativity. Gather a group of people and generate as many ideas as possible on a given topic or problem. The quantity and quality of ideas produced can provide a measure of creative thinking. Brainstorming encourages divergent thinking, allowing participants to explore multiple possibilities without immediate judgement.

During brainstorming sessions, observe how you contribute to the flow of ideas. Do you offer original suggestions? Are you able to build on others' ideas? Do you help steer the group towards innovative solutions? Reflecting on your role in these sessions can reveal your creative thinking style and highlight areas for improvement. Regular participation in brainstorming can also strengthen your creative muscles and improve your ability to think creatively under pressure.

Creativity Tests

Creativity tests, such as the Remote Associates Test (RAT) or the Alternative Uses Test (AUT), are designed to assess specific aspects of creative thinking. The RAT measures convergent thinking, requiring you to find a common link between seemingly unrelated words. The AUT, on the other hand, evaluates divergent thinking by asking you to list as many uses as possible for a common object.

These tests provide structured ways to measure your creativity and compare your performance with normative data. They can help identify specific strengths, such as your ability to make connections or generate multiple ideas, and pinpoint areas that may need further development. Regularly taking creativity tests can track your progress and guide your efforts to enhance your creative thinking skills.

Creative Workshops and Courses

Participating in creative workshops and courses offers a hands-on approach to measuring and developing creativity. These programs often include activities designed to stimulate creative thinking, such as improvisation exercises, design challenges, and collaborative projects. The structured environment and expert guidance provide valuable opportunities to explore and expand your creative abilities.

During these workshops, you receive feedback from instructors and peers, helping you understand your creative strengths and areas for improvement. Engaging in diverse creative activities can also reveal latent talents and interests, encouraging you to pursue new creative avenues. By investing in your creative education, you can build a robust toolkit of skills and techniques to enhance your creativity.

Tracking Progress Over Time

Measuring creativity is not a one-time event but an ongoing process. Tracking your progress over time allows you to see how your creative abilities evolve and improve. Regularly revisit self-assessment tools, performance-based assessments, and feedback from others to gauge your development. Keep a record of your creative achievements and reflect on how your skills have grown.

Setting specific creative goals and monitoring your progress towards them can also be motivating. For example, aim to complete a certain number of creative projects each year, participate in creative challenges, or learn new skills. Regularly reviewing your progress helps you stay focused and committed to your creative growth, providing a sense of accomplishment and direction.

Enhancing Creativity Through Practice

Ultimately, measuring creativity should lead to actions that enhance your creative potential. Engage in regular creative practice, whether through artistic pursuits, problem-solving activities, or innovative projects. Seek out new experiences and challenges that push you out of your comfort zone and stimulate your imagination.

Cultivating a growth mindset is crucial for enhancing creativity. Embrace challenges, view failures as learning opportunities, and persist in your creative efforts. Surround yourself with inspiring people and environments that nurture your creativity. By continually practising and developing your creative skills, you can unlock your full creative potential and achieve remarkable success.

Measuring creativity involves a combination of self-assessment tools, performance-based evaluations, feedback from others, and reflective practices. By understanding and recognising your creative strengths and areas for improvement, you can take proactive steps to enhance your creativity. Regular practice, continuous learning, and a supportive environment are key to developing and sustaining your creative potential. Embrace the journey of measuring and enhancing your creativity, and unlock new possibilities for personal and professional success.

12

Types of Creativity

Creativity is a dynamic and versatile skill that can manifest in various forms across different domains. Understanding the types of creativity can help us appreciate its broad spectrum and apply it effectively in our personal and professional lives. In this chapter, we will explore different types of creativity, providing insights into their unique characteristics and how they contribute to success.

Artistic Creativity

Artistic creativity is perhaps the most recognised form of creativity. It involves expressing oneself through mediums like painting, writing, music, and dance. This type of creativity focuses on the aesthetic and emotive aspects of creation, aiming to evoke emotions and convey messages through artistic expression. Artists use their imagination and skills to create works that can inspire, provoke thought, and connect with people on a deep emotional level.

Measuring artistic creativity can be approached through the evaluation of originality, technical skills, and emotional impact. For instance, in visual arts, one might assess the uniqueness of the artist's style, the complexity of their techniques, and the emotional resonance of their work. In writing, creativity can be measured by examining the innovativeness of the narrative, the richness of the language, and the ability to engage readers emotionally. Peer reviews, competitions, and exhibitions are practical ways to measure and validate artistic creativity.

Scientific Creativity

Scientific creativity involves the generation of new ideas, theories, and solutions within the realm of science and technology. This type of creativity is characterised by curiosity, experimentation, and the ability to see connections between seemingly unrelated phenomena. Scientists and researchers use creative thinking to solve complex problems, develop innovative technologies, and advance our understanding of the natural world.

Measuring scientific creativity can be challenging, but it often involves evaluating the novelty and impact of one's contributions to their field. Publications in reputable journals, patents, and successful research projects are indicators of scientific creativity. Peer reviews and citations also play a crucial role in assessing the significance and originality of scientific work. Recognition through awards and grants can further validate an individual's creative contributions to science.

Entrepreneurial Creativity

Entrepreneurial creativity is about identifying opportunities, developing innovative business ideas, and creating value in the marketplace. Entrepreneurs use creative thinking to design unique products, services, and business models that meet consumer needs and solve problems. This type of creativity requires a blend of vision, risk-taking, and strategic thinking to turn ideas into successful ventures.

Measuring entrepreneurial creativity can be seen through the success and impact of business ventures. Key indicators include the ability to identify market gaps, the innovation in products or services, and the growth and profitability of the business. Customer feedback, market share, and the entrepreneur's ability to adapt to changing market conditions also provide insights into their creative prowess. Recognition through business awards and media coverage can further highlight entrepreneurial creativity.

Social Creativity

Social creativity involves using creative thinking to address social issues and improve communities. This type of creativity is characterised by empathy, collaboration, and a commitment to making a positive impact. Social innovators develop initiatives, programmes, and solutions that tackle challenges such as poverty, education, healthcare, and environmental sustainability.

Measuring social creativity often involves assessing the effectiveness and reach of social initiatives. Key metrics include the number of people impacted, the sustainability of the solutions, and the ability to inspire and mobilise communities. Feedback from beneficiaries, partnerships with other organisations, and recognition through social impact awards can help validate the success of social creativity. The ultimate measure is the tangible improvement in the quality of life for those affected by the initiatives.

Technical Creativity

Technical creativity is about finding innovative solutions to technical problems and improving existing technologies. This type of creativity requires a deep understanding of technical principles and the ability to think outside the box to develop new methods, tools, and systems. Engineers, IT professionals, and inventors often exhibit technical creativity in their work.

Measuring technical creativity can be seen through the development and implementation of new technologies and solutions. Patents, technical papers, and successful projects are indicators of technical creativity. Peer recognition, awards, and the practical impact of one's innovations on industry and society also play a role in assessing technical creativity. The ability to solve complex technical problems efficiently and effectively is a key measure of success in this domain.

Educational Creativity

Educational creativity involves developing innovative teaching methods, curricula, and learning experiences that enhance education. Educators use creative thinking to engage students, foster critical thinking, and make learning more effective and enjoyable. This type of creativity is essential for adapting to the diverse needs of learners and preparing them for a rapidly changing world.

Measuring educational creativity involves evaluating the effectiveness and innovation of teaching practices. Student engagement, feedback, and academic outcomes are indicators of creative teaching methods. Peer reviews, educational research publications, and recognition through teaching awards can also validate an educator's creative contributions. The ultimate measure is the positive impact on students' learning experiences and outcomes.

Cultural Creativity

Cultural creativity is about preserving, promoting, and evolving cultural traditions and expressions. This type of creativity is evident in activities such as storytelling, traditional crafts, music, and dance. Cultural creatives use their skills to keep cultural heritage alive while also adapting it to contemporary contexts.

Measuring cultural creativity can be seen through the preservation and promotion of cultural heritage. Participation in cultural events, exhibitions, and performances are indicators of cultural creativity. Recognition through cultural awards, grants, and community feedback also play a role in validating cultural contributions. The lasting impact on cultural preservation and evolution is a key measure of success in this domain.

Creativity is a multifaceted skill that manifests in various forms across different domains. Understanding the different types of creativity – artistic, scientific, entrepreneurial, social, technical, educational, and cultural – helps us appreciate the broad spectrum of creative potential. By recognising and nurturing these diverse forms of creativity, we can unlock new possibilities for innovation, problem-solving, and personal and professional success. Embrace your creative potential, explore different domains, and contribute to the world in unique and meaningful ways.

13

Identifying and Overcoming Mental Blocks

Mental blocks can stifle creativity and hinder progress, making it challenging to think clearly and solve problems effectively. These barriers can arise from various sources, such as fear, stress, or negative thinking patterns. Understanding how to identify and overcome these mental blocks is crucial for unlocking your creative potential and achieving success. In this chapter, we will explore common types of mental blocks and practical strategies to overcome them.

Understanding Mental Blocks

Mental blocks are psychological barriers that disrupt our thinking processes, making it difficult to generate ideas or find solutions. These blocks can manifest as a lack of motivation, inability to focus, or a pervasive sense of self-doubt. Recognising when you are experiencing a mental block is the first step towards overcoming it. Pay attention to signs such as procrastination, frustration, and feeling overwhelmed, as these can indicate the presence of a mental block.

Mental blocks can be temporary or persistent, depending on their underlying causes. They often result from stress, fear of failure, perfectionism, or negative self-talk. Understanding the root cause of your mental block can help you develop effective strategies to address it. By becoming aware of these barriers, you can take proactive steps to clear your mind and foster a more productive and creative mindset.

Identifying Common Mental Blocks

One of the most common mental blocks is fear of failure. This fear can paralyse you, preventing you from taking risks and exploring new ideas. It often stems from a desire for perfection or a fear of judgement from others. Recognising this fear is essential, as it allows you to confront it directly and reduce its impact on your creativity.

Another common mental block is self-doubt. This involves questioning your abilities and feeling unworthy of success. Self-doubt can erode your confidence and motivation, making it difficult to pursue your goals. Identifying self-doubt involves paying attention to negative thoughts and self-critical attitudes. Once you recognise these patterns, you can work on building your self-esteem and reinforcing positive beliefs about your capabilities.

Overcoming Fear of Failure

To overcome the fear of failure, it's important to shift your perspective. Instead of viewing failure as a negative outcome, see it as a learning opportunity. Understand that mistakes are a natural part of the creative process and that each failure brings you one step closer to success. Embrace a growth mindset, where challenges are seen as chances to develop and improve.

Taking small risks and celebrating incremental successes can also help reduce the fear of failure. Start with manageable tasks and gradually increase the difficulty as your confidence grows. By experiencing success in small steps, you can build resilience and reduce the anxiety associated with taking risks. Surround yourself with supportive people who encourage you and remind you of your strengths and achievements.

Building Self-Confidence

Overcoming self-doubt requires building and maintaining self-confidence. Start by recognising your achievements and strengths. Keep a journal where you record your accomplishments, no matter how small. Reflect on past successes and remind yourself of the skills and qualities that contributed to those achievements. This practice can help shift your focus from your perceived shortcomings to your capabilities and potential.

Positive affirmations can also be powerful tools for building self-confidence. Create a list of affirmations that resonate with you, such as "I am capable," "I trust my abilities," or "I am worthy of success." Repeat these affirmations daily to reinforce a positive self-image. Additionally, seek feedback from trusted peers or mentors who can provide constructive criticism and encourage your growth. Their support can boost your confidence and help you see your potential more clearly.

Managing Stress and Anxiety

Stress and anxiety are significant contributors to mental blocks. Learning to manage these emotions effectively is crucial for maintaining a clear and focused mind. Incorporate stress-relief techniques into your daily routine, such as mindfulness, meditation, or deep-breathing exercises. These practices can help calm your mind, reduce anxiety, and improve your overall well-being.

Physical activity is another excellent way to manage stress. Regular exercise releases endorphins, which are natural mood boosters. Activities like yoga, walking, or swimming can help clear your mind and increase your energy levels. Additionally, ensure you are getting adequate sleep and maintaining a healthy diet, as these factors significantly impact your mental and emotional health. By taking care of your body and mind, you can create a more balanced and resilient state that is conducive to creativity.

Addressing Perfectionism

Perfectionism can be a significant barrier to creativity. The desire to produce flawless work can lead to procrastination and a fear of starting new projects. To overcome perfectionism, it's important to set realistic expectations and recognise that perfection is unattainable. Focus on progress rather than perfection, and give yourself permission to make mistakes and learn from them.

Practising self-compassion is also crucial in addressing perfectionism. Be kind to yourself and acknowledge that everyone has flaws and makes mistakes. Challenge your inner critic by reframing negative thoughts and focusing on your efforts and improvements rather than the final outcome. By adopting a more forgiving attitude towards yourself, you can reduce the pressure to be perfect and allow your creativity to flow more freely.

Cultivating a Positive Mindset

A positive mindset is essential for overcoming mental blocks and fostering creativity. Start by surrounding yourself with positive influences, such as supportive friends, inspiring mentors, and uplifting environments. Engage in activities that bring you joy and fulfilment, as these can boost your mood and enhance your creative thinking.

Gratitude is another powerful tool for cultivating a positive mindset. Practise gratitude by regularly reflecting on the things you are thankful for. Keeping a gratitude journal can help shift your focus from negative thoughts to positive experiences. This practice can improve your overall outlook on life and create a more conducive environment for creativity. Additionally, engage in activities that inspire and energise you, such as reading, listening to music, or spending time in nature.

Seeking Inspiration

Inspiration can help break through mental blocks and ignite your creativity. Expose yourself to new experiences, ideas, and perspectives. Attend workshops, read books, visit museums, or engage in conversations with diverse people. These activities can stimulate your mind and provide fresh insights that spark new ideas.

Additionally, take time to explore your passions and interests. Engage in hobbies or activities that excite you and allow you to express yourself creatively. Whether it's painting, writing, gardening, or playing an instrument, pursuing your interests can rejuvenate your mind and help you overcome creative blocks. By seeking inspiration in various forms, you can keep your creativity alive and thriving.

Setting Clear Goals

Setting clear and achievable goals can help you overcome mental blocks and maintain focus. Break down larger projects into smaller, manageable tasks, and create a timeline for completing them. This approach can reduce feelings of overwhelm and provide a clear path forward. Celebrate your progress along the way to stay motivated and encouraged.

Visualising your goals can also be a powerful tool for overcoming mental blocks. Create a vision board or write down your goals and place them where you can see them daily. This constant reminder can keep you focused and motivated. Additionally, setting SMART (Specific, Measurable, Achievable, Relevant, Time-bound) goals can help you stay organised and ensure that your objectives are realistic and attainable.

Building a Support Network

Having a strong support network is crucial for overcoming mental blocks. Surround yourself with people who encourage and motivate you. Share your challenges and successes with them, and seek their advice when needed. A supportive network can provide valuable feedback, fresh perspectives, and emotional support, helping you stay resilient and focused on your goals.

Joining creative communities or groups can also be beneficial. These communities provide a platform for sharing ideas, collaborating on projects, and receiving constructive feedback. Being part of a community of like-minded individuals can inspire you, boost your confidence, and help you overcome creative blocks. Whether online or in-person, these connections can play a significant role in your creative journey.

Identifying and overcoming mental blocks is essential for unlocking your creative potential and achieving success. By understanding common mental blocks, such as fear of failure, self-doubt, stress, and perfectionism, you can develop effective strategies to address them. Cultivating a positive mindset, seeking inspiration, setting clear goals, building a support network, and practising mindfulness are all powerful tools for overcoming mental barriers. Embrace these strategies and take proactive steps to clear your mind, enhance your creativity, and achieve your goals.

14

Techniques to Stimulate Creative Thinking

Creative thinking is a valuable skill that can enhance problem-solving, innovation, and personal expression. Whether you're tackling a work project, solving a personal challenge, or simply seeking new ideas, stimulating your creativity can lead to remarkable outcomes. In this chapter, we will explore various techniques to stimulate creative thinking, helping you unlock your potential and achieve success.

Brainstorming

Brainstorming is one of the most effective techniques for generating a wealth of ideas quickly. It involves free thinking and open discussion, where every idea is welcomed without immediate criticism or judgment. This process encourages divergent thinking, allowing you to explore multiple possibilities and perspectives. To start a brainstorming session, gather a group of people or work alone, set a clear objective, and begin generating ideas. The goal is to come up with as many ideas as possible, no matter how unconventional they may seem.

During brainstorming sessions, it's essential to create an environment where everyone feels comfortable sharing their thoughts. Encourage wild ideas and build on the suggestions of others. Writing down all the ideas on a whiteboard or a large sheet of paper can help visualise the creative process. After the initial session, review and refine the ideas, combining them if necessary, to form practical and innovative solutions. Regular brainstorming sessions can keep your creativity sharp and responsive.

Mind Mapping

Mind mapping is a visual technique that helps organise and connect ideas. It starts with a central concept, from which related ideas branch out in all directions. This method mimics the way our brains naturally think, making it easier to see relationships and patterns between different ideas. To create a mind map, start with a central idea and draw branches to represent related concepts. Add sub-branches to further explore each concept, and use colours and images to make the map more engaging and memorable.

Mind mapping can be particularly useful for complex projects or problems, as it allows you to break down the issue into manageable parts and see the bigger picture simultaneously. This technique encourages both linear and non-linear thinking, enabling you to explore different angles and connections. By visually mapping out your thoughts, you can identify gaps, generate new ideas, and develop more comprehensive solutions.

SCAMPER Technique

The SCAMPER technique is a structured method for creative thinking that involves seven different approaches to generate ideas: Substitute, Combine, Adapt, Modify, Put to another use, Eliminate, and Rearrange. Each approach encourages you to look at a problem or idea from a different perspective, helping you think outside the box. To use SCAMPER, start with a specific challenge or idea and apply each of the seven prompts to explore new possibilities.

For example, if you are trying to improve a product, you might ask: "What can I substitute in this product to make it better?" or "How can I combine different features to create something new?" By systematically applying each prompt, you can uncover a wide range of innovative ideas. The SCAMPER technique helps break habitual thinking patterns and opens up new avenues for creative solutions.

Role-Playing

Role-playing involves stepping into the shoes of another person to gain a different perspective. This technique can be particularly useful for understanding the needs and preferences of others, such as customers, clients, or stakeholders. To use role-playing, identify a specific role related to your challenge, such as a customer, competitor, or colleague. Then, imagine how they would approach the situation, what challenges they might face, and what solutions they might consider.

By adopting different roles, you can uncover insights and ideas that you might not have considered from your usual perspective. Role-playing encourages empathy and helps you see the problem through fresh eyes. It can also reveal hidden opportunities and inspire innovative solutions that address the needs of various stakeholders.

Random Word Association

Random word association is a technique that involves using random words to spark new ideas and connections. This method helps break free from conventional thinking patterns and encourages creative exploration. To use this technique, choose a random word from a dictionary or word generator. Then, brainstorm how this word relates to your challenge or idea, and see what new thoughts emerge.

For instance, if your challenge is to develop a new marketing strategy and the random word is "tree," you might think about growth, branches, roots, and leaves. These associations could lead to ideas such as branching out into new markets, rooting your strategy in strong values, or developing a campaign that emphasises growth and sustainability. Random word association helps you think laterally and explore unexpected connections.

Changing Your Environment

Sometimes, a change of scenery can stimulate creative thinking. Our environment significantly impacts our mood and thought processes, and a fresh setting can provide new stimuli and inspiration. If you're feeling stuck, try working in a different location, such as a park, café, or co-working space. The new sights, sounds, and atmosphere can help you break out of routine thinking and see your challenge from a different perspective.

Additionally, surrounding yourself with inspiring objects, artwork, or natural elements can boost creativity. Create a workspace that reflects your interests and stimulates your senses. Incorporate colours, textures, and materials that you find engaging and motivating. By altering your environment, you can create a more dynamic and inspiring space for creative thinking.

Mindfulness and Meditation

Mindfulness and meditation are powerful tools for clearing your mind and enhancing focus. These practices help reduce stress and mental clutter, allowing you to think more clearly and creatively. Mindfulness involves paying attention to the present moment without judgment, while meditation typically involves focused breathing or guided visualisation. Incorporating these practices into your daily routine can improve your overall mental well-being and creativity.

Even short mindfulness exercises, such as deep breathing or a five-minute meditation session, can have a significant impact on your creativity. These practices help quiet the mind, making it easier to connect with your inner thoughts and generate new ideas. Regular mindfulness and meditation can enhance your ability to stay present, improve concentration, and open up new pathways for creative thinking.

Collaboration and Networking

Collaborating with others and expanding your network can stimulate creative thinking. Engaging with people who have different perspectives, backgrounds, and expertise can introduce you to new ideas and approaches. Participate in group discussions, brainstorming sessions, and collaborative projects to benefit from the collective creativity of the group.

Networking events, workshops, and conferences are also great opportunities to connect with like-minded individuals and exchange ideas. By building a diverse network, you can gain access to a wide range of insights and inspiration. Collaboration and networking encourage the sharing of knowledge and foster a supportive environment where creative thinking can thrive.

Keeping a Creativity Journal

A creativity journal is a personal space where you can capture your thoughts, ideas, and inspirations. Regularly writing in a journal helps you track your creative process and reflect on your progress. Use your journal to jot down new ideas, brainstorm solutions, and explore different perspectives. You can also use it to record quotes, images, or experiences that inspire you.

Keeping a creativity journal encourages consistent creative practice and helps you develop a habit of thinking creatively.

Reviewing your entries can reveal patterns and connections that you might not have noticed initially. This reflective practice can enhance your self-awareness and provide valuable insights into your creative journey.

Embracing Playfulness

Playfulness is an essential component of creativity. Approaching tasks with a playful attitude can reduce pressure and open up new possibilities. Engage in activities that you enjoy and that stimulate your imagination, such as drawing, playing games, or exploring new hobbies. Playfulness encourages experimentation and risk-taking, which are crucial for generating innovative ideas.

Incorporate elements of play into your work routine, such as taking short breaks to engage in a fun activity or using playful methods to brainstorm ideas. Allowing yourself to play can relieve stress and boost your energy levels, making it easier to approach challenges with a fresh perspective. Embracing playfulness can rejuvenate your mind and enhance your creative thinking.

Stimulating creative thinking involves adopting various techniques that encourage new perspectives and innovative ideas. From brainstorming and mind mapping to mindfulness and playfulness, these methods can help you break free from conventional thinking patterns and unlock your creative potential. By incorporating these techniques into your daily routine, you can enhance your problem-solving skills, foster innovation, and achieve greater success. Embrace these strategies and watch your creativity flourish.

15

Daily Habits to Nurture Creativity

Creativity is a valuable skill that can be cultivated through daily habits. By incorporating specific routines and practices into your everyday life, you can enhance your creative thinking and unlock your full potential. In this chapter, we will explore various daily habits that can nurture and sustain your creativity, helping you achieve greater success and fulfilment.

Morning Pages

One effective habit to nurture creativity is writing morning pages. This practice involves writing three pages of free-form, stream-of-consciousness writing first thing in the morning. The idea is to clear your mind of clutter and allow your thoughts to flow freely onto the page. This can help you process emotions, clarify ideas, and stimulate creative thinking.

Morning pages are not meant to be polished or perfect; they are simply a way to unlock your thoughts and get your creative juices flowing. By making this a daily habit, you can start your day with a clear mind and a fresh perspective. Over time, you may find that your morning pages become a source of inspiration and a valuable tool for generating new ideas.

Reading Regularly

Reading is a powerful habit that can greatly enhance your creativity. By exposing yourself to different ideas, perspectives, and writing styles, you can expand your knowledge and stimulate your imagination. Make it a habit to read regularly, whether it's books, articles, or blogs on topics that interest you.

Diversifying your reading material can also boost your creativity. Explore genres and subjects outside your usual preferences to gain new insights and inspiration. Whether you're reading fiction, non-fiction, poetry, or scientific articles, the act of reading can spark new ideas and help you see the world from different angles. Set aside dedicated time each day for reading, and let the words ignite your creative mind.

Keeping a Creativity Journal

A creativity journal is a personal space where you can capture your thoughts, ideas, and inspirations. Make it a habit to write in your journal every day, jotting down anything that sparks your interest or imagination. This could include new ideas, reflections on your day, or even sketches and doodles.

Regularly writing in a creativity journal helps you track your creative process and reflect on your progress. Reviewing your entries can reveal patterns and connections that you might not have noticed initially. This reflective practice can enhance your self-awareness and provide valuable insights into your creative journey. Your journal can become a treasure trove of inspiration, fueling your creative projects and endeavours.

Engaging in Physical Activity

Physical activity is not only good for your body but also beneficial for your mind. Regular exercise can boost your creativity by increasing blood flow to the brain and releasing endorphins, which enhance your mood and energy levels. Whether it's walking, running, yoga, or dancing, find a form of physical activity that you enjoy and make it a daily habit.

Incorporating movement into your daily routine can help you break free from mental blocks and stimulate creative thinking. Physical activity provides a break from routine tasks and allows your mind to wander, often leading to new ideas and solutions. Make time for exercise each day, and notice how it enhances your overall well-being and creative abilities.

Seeking Inspiration

Inspiration can come from many sources, and actively seeking it out can nurture your creativity. Make it a habit to expose yourself to new experiences, ideas, and perspectives. Visit museums, attend workshops, explore nature, or engage in conversations with diverse people. These activities can provide fresh stimuli and ignite your imagination.

Keep an open mind and be curious about the world around you. Carry a notebook or use your phone to capture moments of inspiration as they happen. Whether it's a beautiful scene, an interesting conversation, or a thought-provoking piece of art, these moments can serve as fuel for your creative projects. By seeking inspiration daily, you can keep your creative mind active and engaged.

Setting Aside Time for Creative Activities

Dedicating time each day to creative activities is essential for nurturing creativity. Whether it's writing, drawing, playing an instrument, or crafting, find an activity that you enjoy and make it a regular part of your routine. Consistent practice helps you develop your skills and keeps your creativity flowing.

Set aside a specific time each day for your chosen creative activity. Treat this time as sacred and free from distractions. Allow yourself to experiment and explore without worrying about the outcome. The more you engage in creative activities, the more you will build confidence in your abilities and expand your creative horizons.

Embracing Playfulness

Playfulness is a key component of creativity. Approaching tasks with a playful attitude can reduce pressure and open up new possibilities. Make time for activities that bring you joy and allow you to express yourself freely, such as playing games, experimenting with new hobbies, or engaging in light-hearted creative projects.

Incorporate elements of play into your daily routine, even in small ways. Take short breaks to engage in a fun activity or use playful methods to brainstorm ideas. Embracing playfulness can relieve stress and boost your energy levels, making it easier to approach challenges with a fresh perspective. By making play a daily habit, you can keep your creative spirit alive and thriving.

Connecting with Like-Minded Individuals

Surrounding yourself with like-minded individuals can provide support, motivation, and inspiration. Make it a habit to connect with people who share your interests and passions. Join creative communities, attend networking events, or participate in online forums where you can exchange ideas and collaborate on projects.

Engaging with a supportive network can help you stay motivated and inspired. Share your creative journey with others, seek feedback, and offer support in return. Collaboration and discussion can lead to new insights and ideas, enhancing your creative thinking. By building and nurturing these connections, you can create a vibrant and inspiring environment for your creativity to flourish.

Practising Gratitude

Gratitude is a powerful habit that can enhance your overall well-being and creativity. Taking time each day to reflect on what you are thankful for can shift your focus from negative thoughts to positive experiences. This practice can improve your mood, increase your resilience, and create a more positive mindset for creative thinking.

Keep a gratitude journal where you write down three things you are grateful for each day. These can be simple pleasures, personal achievements, or moments of kindness. Reflecting on these positive aspects of your life can boost your happiness and open your mind to new possibilities. By practising gratitude daily, you can cultivate a more optimistic and creative outlook.

Limiting Screen Time

Excessive screen time can hinder creativity by causing distractions and mental fatigue. Make a conscious effort to limit your screen time, especially on social media and entertainment platforms. Instead, use your free time for activities that stimulate your mind and encourage creative thinking.

Set boundaries for your screen use, such as designated times for checking emails or browsing social media. Create tech-free zones or periods during your day where you focus on offline activities. By reducing screen time, you can free up mental space for creative ideas and engage more deeply with your surroundings and projects.

Nurturing creativity requires consistent effort and the incorporation of specific daily habits. By practising morning pages, reading regularly, engaging in mindfulness, keeping a creativity journal, staying physically active, seeking inspiration, dedicating time to creative activities, embracing playfulness, connecting with like-minded individuals, practising gratitude, and limiting screen time, you can cultivate a more creative and fulfilling life. Embrace these habits and watch your creativity flourish, leading to greater success and personal satisfaction.

16

Creative Problem-Solving in Everyday Situations

Creative problem-solving is an invaluable skill that can transform how we approach everyday challenges. By thinking outside the box, we can find innovative solutions to common problems, enhancing our efficiency, productivity, and overall satisfaction. In this chapter, we will explore various strategies for applying creative problem-solving in everyday situations, helping you unlock your potential for creative thinking and success.

Understanding Creative Problem-Solving

Creative problem-solving involves approaching challenges in novel and imaginative ways. It goes beyond conventional thinking and encourages us to explore new perspectives, make unique connections, and develop innovative solutions. This type of problem-solving is not just for artists or inventors; it is a practical skill that can be applied in all areas of life, from work to home to personal projects.

To start, it's essential to adopt a mindset that embraces creativity and open-mindedness. Recognise that every problem has multiple solutions and be willing to explore different approaches. This mindset sets the stage for effective creative problem-solving, allowing you to navigate everyday challenges with confidence and ingenuity.

Embracing a Positive Attitude

A positive attitude is crucial for creative problem-solving. When faced with a challenge, it's easy to become frustrated or discouraged. However, maintaining a positive outlook can help you stay motivated and open to new ideas. Believe in your ability to find solutions and approach each problem as an opportunity for growth and learning.

To cultivate a positive attitude, practice gratitude and mindfulness. Focus on the aspects of your life that are going well and remind yourself of past successes. Mindfulness can help you stay present and reduce stress, making it easier to think clearly and creatively. By maintaining a positive attitude, you create a mental environment conducive to innovative thinking.

Breaking Down the Problem

One effective strategy for creative problem-solving is breaking down the problem into smaller, manageable parts. This approach allows you to focus on specific aspects of the issue, making it less overwhelming and easier to tackle. Start by identifying the main problem and then list all the smaller components or contributing factors.

For example, if you're struggling with time management, break down the problem into tasks such as prioritising activities, setting realistic deadlines, and eliminating distractions. By addressing each component separately, you can develop targeted solutions that collectively resolve the larger issue. This method not only simplifies the problem but also provides a clear path to follow, enhancing your ability to find creative solutions.

Brainstorming Solutions

Brainstorming is a powerful tool for generating a wide range of potential solutions. Set aside dedicated time for brainstorming and encourage free thinking without judgment or criticism. Write down all ideas, no matter how unconventional they may seem. The goal is to create a large pool of possibilities to explore further.

Once you have a list of ideas, evaluate each one for feasibility and potential impact. Combine or modify ideas to enhance their effectiveness. This process helps you discover innovative solutions that you might not have considered initially. Regular brainstorming sessions can keep your problem-solving skills sharp and responsive.

Using Analogies and Metaphors

Analogies and metaphors can provide fresh perspectives on problems, making it easier to find creative solutions. By comparing your problem to a different situation or concept, you can uncover similarities and insights that lead to innovative ideas. This technique helps you think outside the box and approach challenges from new angles.

For instance, if you're trying to improve teamwork in your office, you might compare your team to a sports team. Consider how athletes work together, communicate, and support each other to achieve their goals. Applying these principles to your workplace can inspire new strategies for enhancing collaboration and productivity. Using analogies and metaphors encourages lateral thinking, expanding your problem-solving toolkit.

Seeking Diverse Perspectives

Diverse perspectives can significantly enhance creative problem-solving. When you involve people with different backgrounds, experiences, and viewpoints, you gain access to a broader range of ideas and solutions. Seek input from colleagues, friends, or family members who can offer unique insights into your problem.

Collaboration is key to harnessing the power of diverse perspectives. Encourage open dialogue and active listening to understand different viewpoints fully. This inclusive approach fosters a collaborative environment where innovative ideas can flourish. By valuing and integrating diverse perspectives, you can develop more comprehensive and effective solutions to everyday challenges.

Practising Lateral Thinking

Lateral thinking involves looking at problems from unconventional angles and making connections that aren't immediately obvious. This technique encourages you to step away from traditional linear thinking and explore more creative pathways. Practising lateral thinking can help you uncover hidden opportunities and develop innovative solutions.

To practise lateral thinking, try reversing assumptions about the problem, asking "what if" questions, or using random stimuli to inspire new ideas. For example, if you're trying to improve customer service, you might ask, "What if our customers could design their ideal service experience?" This question can lead to new insights and approaches that enhance customer satisfaction. By regularly practising lateral thinking, you can develop a more flexible and creative mindset.

Implementing Small Changes

Implementing small changes can lead to significant improvements over time. Instead of trying to solve a problem with one large solution, break it down into smaller, manageable steps.

This approach allows you to test ideas, make adjustments, and gradually build towards a comprehensive solution.

For instance, if you're looking to improve your daily productivity, start by implementing small changes such as adjusting your morning routine, setting specific goals for the day, or minimising distractions during work hours. Evaluate the impact of each change and refine your approach as needed. This iterative process helps you find effective solutions and build momentum towards larger goals.

Learning from Failure

Failure is an inevitable part of the creative problem-solving process. Instead of viewing failure as a setback, see it as a valuable learning opportunity. Analyse what went wrong, identify lessons learned, and use this knowledge to improve your approach. Embracing failure with a growth mindset can enhance your resilience and creativity.

To learn from failure, keep a record of your attempts and their outcomes. Reflect on what worked, what didn't, and why. This practice helps you identify patterns and develop better strategies for future challenges. By viewing failure as a stepping stone to success, you can maintain a positive attitude and continue pushing the boundaries of your creative problem-solving abilities.

Keeping an Open Mind

An open mind is essential for creative problem-solving. Be willing to explore new ideas, even if they seem unconventional or risky. Avoid dismissing ideas too quickly and give yourself the freedom to experiment and innovate. An open-minded approach encourages curiosity and fosters a culture of continuous improvement.

To cultivate an open mind, practice active listening and seek out diverse sources of inspiration. Engage with people who challenge your thinking and expose yourself to new experiences and perspectives. By staying open to new ideas and possibilities, you can enhance your ability to find creative solutions to everyday problems.

Developing a Routine

Consistency is key to nurturing creative problem-solving skills. Develop a routine that incorporates regular time for creative thinking and problem-solving activities. This routine can include practices such as brainstorming sessions, reading, journaling, and mindfulness exercises. By making creative problem-solving a daily habit, you can keep your mind sharp and responsive.

Set aside specific times each day or week for focused creative thinking. Treat this time as a priority, free from distractions and interruptions. Over time, this routine will help you build and maintain strong problem-solving skills, enabling you to tackle everyday challenges with confidence and creativity.

Creative problem-solving is a valuable skill that can transform how you approach everyday challenges. By adopting strategies such as embracing a positive attitude, breaking down problems, brainstorming, using analogies, seeking diverse perspectives, practising lateral thinking, implementing small changes, learning from failure, keeping an open mind, and developing a routine, you can enhance your ability to find innovative solutions. Embrace these techniques and watch your problem-solving skills flourish, leading to greater success and personal fulfilment.

17

Enhancing Personal Relationships through Creativity

Creativity is not only a tool for professional success but also a powerful way to enrich personal relationships. By applying creative thinking and actions to how we interact with others, we can build stronger, more fulfilling connections. In this chapter, we will explore various ways to enhance personal relationships through creativity, offering practical tips and strategies to deepen bonds and improve communication.

Creative Communication

Effective communication is the foundation of any strong relationship. Adding creativity to your communication can make interactions more engaging and meaningful. Instead of sticking to routine conversations, try to introduce new topics, ask thought-provoking questions, and share interesting stories. This approach keeps the dialogue fresh and exciting, encouraging deeper connections.

Using creative methods to express yourself can also enhance communication. Write letters, leave thoughtful notes, or send personalised messages. These small gestures show that you care and are willing to go the extra mile to communicate your feelings. By being inventive in how you communicate, you can foster a more open and dynamic relationship.

Planning Unique Experiences

Shared experiences are crucial for building and maintaining strong relationships. Instead of sticking to the usual outings, plan unique and memorable activities that you both enjoy. This could be anything from a surprise picnic in a scenic location to a themed dinner night at home. The key is to think outside the box and create moments that you will both cherish.

Involving your partner or friend in the planning process can also be a fun and collaborative activity. Brainstorm together to come up with creative ideas for your next adventure. This not only strengthens your bond but also ensures that the experience is enjoyable for both of you. By regularly introducing new and exciting activities, you can keep the relationship vibrant and full of positive memories.

Creative Problem-Solving in Relationships

Every relationship faces challenges, but using creative problem-solving can help navigate these difficulties effectively. When disagreements arise, try to approach them with an open mind and a willingness to find innovative solutions. Instead of focusing on the problem, work together to brainstorm potential solutions. This collaborative approach can lead to more effective and harmonious resolutions.

For example, if you and your partner have different opinions on how to spend your free time, create a list of activities you both enjoy and take turns choosing from it. This ensures that both parties feel valued and heard. By applying creative problem-solving techniques, you can address conflicts in a way that strengthens rather than strains the relationship.

Celebrating Achievements and Milestones

Celebrating achievements and milestones creatively can add a special touch to your relationship. Whether it's a birthday, anniversary, or personal accomplishment, find unique ways to mark the occasion. This could be through personalised gifts, surprise parties, or creating a scrapbook of shared memories. The effort you put into these celebrations shows your appreciation and love.

Personalised celebrations make the other person feel special and valued. Consider their interests and preferences when planning these events. For example, if your friend loves art, organise a private painting session or visit a local gallery together. By tailoring celebrations to the individual, you create meaningful experiences that deepen your bond.

Fostering Shared Interests

Cultivating shared interests is an excellent way to enhance personal relationships. Engage in activities that you both enjoy, such as cooking, gardening, or playing sports. These shared hobbies provide opportunities for quality time together and can lead to deeper connections. Explore new interests together as well, which can be an exciting journey of discovery for both of you.

If you don't already have shared interests, try to find common ground by experimenting with different activities. Attend workshops, take classes, or volunteer together. These experiences can reveal new passions and create lasting memories. By investing time in shared interests, you build a stronger foundation for your relationship.

Expressing Gratitude Creatively

Expressing gratitude is a powerful way to strengthen relationships. Instead of simply saying "thank you," find creative ways to show your appreciation. This could be through handwritten notes, thoughtful gestures, or surprise gifts. These acts of gratitude demonstrate that you value and appreciate the other person, which can deepen your connection.

For example, you could create a gratitude jar where you regularly add notes of appreciation for your partner or friend. Reading these notes together can be a heartwarming experience that reinforces your bond. By regularly expressing gratitude in creative ways, you nurture a positive and supportive relationship.

Enhancing Emotional Intelligence

Emotional intelligence plays a crucial role in personal relationships. Being aware of and understanding your own emotions, as well as those of others, can improve communication and empathy. Practice active listening, validate each other's feelings, and respond with compassion and understanding. These skills can be developed and enhanced through creative exercises such as role-playing and journaling.

Role-playing different scenarios can help you see situations from the other person's perspective, fostering empathy and understanding. Journaling about your emotions and experiences allows you to reflect on your interactions and identify areas for improvement. By enhancing your emotional intelligence, you can create a more empathetic and supportive relationship.

Building Trust through Creativity

Trust is the cornerstone of any healthy relationship. Building and maintaining trust requires consistency, honesty, and effort.

Creative activities can help reinforce trust by showing your commitment and reliability. For example, create a joint vision board with your partner or friend to visualise your shared goals and aspirations. This collaborative project can strengthen your bond and build mutual trust.

Another way to build trust is by setting and achieving small goals together. Whether it's completing a DIY project, planning a trip, or starting a new hobby, working towards a common goal reinforces your reliability and teamwork. Celebrating these achievements together can further solidify the trust in your relationship.

Encouraging Personal Growth

Supporting each other's personal growth is a vital aspect of a strong relationship. Encourage your partner or friend to pursue their passions and interests, and be their biggest cheerleader. Engage in activities that promote self-improvement and learning, such as attending workshops, reading books, or taking up new hobbies together.

Creative activities can also foster personal growth. For instance, try creative writing exercises to explore your thoughts and emotions, or take an art class to express yourself in new ways. By supporting each other's growth and development, you create a relationship that is dynamic and fulfilling.

Creating Rituals and Traditions

Rituals and traditions provide a sense of stability and continuity in relationships. These can be as simple as a weekly movie night or as elaborate as an annual trip. Creating and maintaining these rituals together fosters a sense of belonging and shared history. Be creative in establishing new traditions that reflect your unique bond.

For example, you could start a tradition of cooking a special meal together every Sunday or having a monthly "book club" where you discuss a book you both read. These rituals become cherished moments that strengthen your connection and create lasting memories. By embedding creativity into your traditions, you ensure they remain engaging and meaningful.

Practising Forgiveness

Forgiveness is essential for maintaining healthy relationships. Holding onto grudges and resentments can create barriers and strain your connection. Practising forgiveness involves letting go of past hurts and focusing on moving forward together. Creative exercises such as writing a forgiveness letter or creating a symbolic gesture can help facilitate this process.

Writing a forgiveness letter allows you to express your feelings and release negative emotions. You don't necessarily have to share the letter; the act of writing can be therapeutic in itself. Similarly, creating a symbolic gesture, such as planting a tree together to represent a new beginning, can help you both move past conflicts and strengthen your bond. By practising forgiveness, you can maintain a positive and resilient relationship.

Enhancing personal relationships through creativity involves incorporating creative thinking and actions into your interactions. By engaging in creative communication, planning unique experiences, solving problems together, celebrating achievements, fostering shared interests, expressing gratitude, enhancing emotional intelligence, building trust, encouraging personal growth, creating rituals, and practising forgiveness, you can build stronger and more fulfilling connections. Embrace these creative strategies to enrich your relationships and enjoy deeper, more meaningful bonds with the people you care about.

18

Creative Hobbies and Their Benefits

Engaging in creative hobbies is a wonderful way to nurture your mind, explore new talents, and enhance your overall well-being. Creative activities not only provide a fun and fulfilling pastime but also offer numerous mental, emotional, and even physical benefits. In this chapter, we will explore various creative hobbies and their benefits, helping you find activities that inspire and enrich your life.

Painting and Drawing

Painting and drawing are timeless creative hobbies that allow for self-expression and relaxation. These activities enable you to capture your thoughts, emotions, and observations on paper or canvas. Whether you prefer watercolours, acrylics, pencils, or charcoal, the act of creating visual art can be incredibly therapeutic and satisfying.

Engaging in painting and drawing enhances your fine motor skills and improves hand-eye coordination. It also stimulates the brain, encouraging the development of new neural connections. Additionally, creating art can be a meditative practice, helping to reduce stress and promote mindfulness. By focusing on your artwork, you can achieve a state of flow, where time seems to stand still, and you become fully immersed in the creative process.

Writing

Writing is a versatile hobby that encompasses a wide range of activities, from journaling and poetry to storytelling and blogging. It allows you to articulate your thoughts, share your experiences, and explore your imagination. Writing can be a solitary pursuit or a collaborative effort, making it adaptable to different preferences and lifestyles.

The benefits of writing are numerous. It enhances your communication skills, boosts your vocabulary, and improves your ability to organise and express ideas clearly. Writing can also be a powerful tool for self-reflection and emotional processing. By putting your thoughts and feelings into words, you can gain clarity and insight into your experiences. Additionally, writing can serve as a creative outlet, providing a sense of accomplishment and personal fulfilment.

Playing a Musical Instrument

Learning to play a musical instrument is a highly rewarding creative hobby that offers both cognitive and emotional benefits. Whether you choose the piano, guitar, violin, or any other instrument, the process of learning and playing music engages various parts of the brain, enhancing your memory, coordination, and concentration.

Playing a musical instrument also fosters patience and discipline, as it requires regular practice and perseverance. The emotional benefits are equally significant; music can be a powerful means of self-expression and a way to connect with others. Performing music, whether alone or in a group, can boost your confidence and provide a sense of accomplishment. Additionally, music has been shown to reduce stress and anxiety, promoting overall mental well-being.

Cooking and Baking

Cooking and baking are creative hobbies that not only satisfy your culinary cravings but also stimulate your creativity and problem-solving skills. Experimenting with new recipes, ingredients, and techniques allows you to express yourself through food and discover new flavours and combinations. Cooking can be a solo activity or a social one, making it a versatile and enjoyable hobby.

The benefits of cooking and baking extend beyond the kitchen. These activities can improve your planning and organisational skills, as you need to follow recipes, measure ingredients, and manage time effectively. Cooking at home also encourages healthier eating habits and a greater appreciation for the food you consume. Additionally, sharing your culinary creations with family and friends can strengthen relationships and create lasting memories.

Gardening

Gardening is a fulfilling hobby that connects you with nature and provides a sense of accomplishment. Whether you have a small balcony garden or a large backyard, tending to plants, flowers, and vegetables can be incredibly rewarding. Gardening requires patience, care, and creativity, as you design and maintain your green space.

The physical benefits of gardening are significant, as it involves various forms of exercise, such as digging, planting, and weeding. These activities can improve your strength, flexibility, and overall fitness. Gardening also has mental health benefits; it can reduce stress, promote relaxation, and provide a sense of purpose. The act of nurturing plants and watching them grow can be deeply satisfying and boost your overall well-being.

Photography

Photography is a creative hobby that allows you to capture and preserve moments, landscapes, and experiences through the lens of a camera. Whether you use a professional camera or a smartphone, photography encourages you to observe the world around you more closely and appreciate its beauty and diversity.

Engaging in photography can improve your visual perception and attention to detail. It also encourages you to explore different perspectives and experiment with composition, lighting, and angles. Photography can be a solitary activity or a social one, as you can join photography clubs, participate in workshops, or share your work online. The process of creating and sharing your photos can provide a sense of achievement and connect you with a community of like-minded individuals.

Crafting

Crafting encompasses a wide range of activities, from knitting and crocheting to scrapbooking and jewellery making. These hobbies allow you to create beautiful and functional items with your hands, using various materials and techniques. Crafting can be a relaxing and meditative activity, providing a break from the stresses of daily life.

The benefits of crafting are numerous. It improves your fine motor skills, hand-eye coordination, and attention to detail. Crafting also stimulates your creativity and problem-solving abilities, as you design and execute your projects. Additionally, creating handmade items can provide a sense of accomplishment and pride.

Crafting can be a social activity as well, offering opportunities to connect with others through craft groups, workshops, and online communities.

Dance

Dance is a dynamic and expressive hobby that combines physical movement with creativity. Whether you prefer ballet, hip-hop, salsa, or contemporary dance, moving to music allows you to express yourself and experience the joy of rhythmic movement. Dance can be practiced alone, in a class, or as part of a performance group, making it a versatile and inclusive activity.

The physical benefits of dance are well-documented; it improves cardiovascular health, strength, flexibility, and coordination. Dance also has significant mental and emotional benefits. It can boost your mood, reduce stress, and increase your self-confidence. The social aspects of dance, such as attending classes or participating in dance events, can help you build connections and foster a sense of community.

Pottery and Ceramics

Pottery and ceramics are tactile and creative hobbies that involve shaping and moulding clay into functional or decorative objects. These activities require patience, precision, and creativity, as you transform raw materials into finished pieces. Working with clay can be a deeply satisfying and meditative process, allowing you to focus your mind and express your artistic vision.

The benefits of pottery and ceramics include improved hand-eye coordination, fine motor skills, and attention to detail. These activities also stimulate your creativity and problem-solving abilities, as you design and create your pieces. Additionally, working with clay can be therapeutic, reducing stress and promoting relaxation. The sense of accomplishment that comes from creating a finished piece of pottery or ceramics can boost your confidence and provide a lasting sense of pride.

Theatre and Drama

Engaging in theatre and drama is a highly creative hobby that involves acting, scriptwriting, directing, or stage design. Participating in theatrical productions allows you to explore different characters, stories, and emotions, providing a powerful means of self-expression and communication. Theatre and drama can be practiced in a group setting, fostering collaboration and teamwork.

The benefits of theatre and drama extend beyond the stage. These activities improve your public speaking, communication, and interpersonal skills. They also enhance your empathy and emotional intelligence, as you step into the shoes of different characters and explore their experiences. Participating in theatre and drama can boost your confidence and self-esteem, providing a sense of achievement and belonging. The collaborative nature of theatre fosters strong connections and a sense of community among participants.

Creative hobbies offer a wealth of benefits that enhance your mental, emotional, and physical well-being. Whether you choose to paint, write, play music, cook, garden, take photos, craft, dance, work with clay, or engage in theatre, these activities provide opportunities for self-expression, relaxation, and personal growth. By incorporating creative hobbies into your daily life, you can unlock your potential, find joy in the creative process, and enrich your overall quality of life. Embrace the world of creative hobbies and discover the many ways they can contribute to your success and fulfilment.

19

Fostering a Creative Environment at Work

A creative work environment can significantly enhance productivity, innovation, and job satisfaction. By fostering creativity in the workplace, you can encourage employees to think outside the box, develop innovative solutions, and feel more engaged with their work. In this chapter, we will explore various strategies to create and maintain a creative environment at work, helping you unlock the full potential of your team.

Encouraging Open Communication

Open communication is the foundation of a creative workplace. When employees feel comfortable sharing their ideas and opinions, they are more likely to contribute innovative solutions. Create an atmosphere where everyone feels valued and heard by encouraging regular team meetings, brainstorming sessions, and open forums for discussion. This helps to build trust and collaboration among team members.

It's essential to actively listen to your employees and show appreciation for their input. Acknowledge their contributions, provide constructive feedback, and encourage them to expand on their ideas. By fostering a culture of open communication, you create a safe space for creativity to flourish. Regularly soliciting feedback and suggestions from your team can also provide valuable insights and drive continuous improvement.

Additionally, ensure that communication channels are accessible and inclusive. Use various methods, such as face-to-face meetings, emails, and digital collaboration tools, to cater to different communication preferences. By making it easy for employees to share their thoughts, you can capture a diverse range of ideas and perspectives, which can lead to more innovative solutions.

Providing a Flexible Work Environment

A flexible work environment can significantly enhance creativity. Allowing employees to choose their work hours, work remotely, or take breaks when needed can help them manage their time more effectively and reduce stress. Flexibility enables employees to work when they feel most productive and inspired, leading to higher quality work and increased innovation.

Implementing a results-oriented work environment (ROWE) can be beneficial. In a ROWE, employees are evaluated based on their output rather than the number of hours they spend in the office. This approach encourages employees to focus on achieving their goals and finding creative ways to meet their objectives. It also fosters a sense of autonomy and ownership, which can boost motivation and job satisfaction.

Providing a variety of workspaces within the office can also support flexibility. Create different zones for focused work, collaboration, and relaxation. This allows employees to choose the environment that best suits their current task and mood. By offering flexibility in how and where employees work, you can create a more dynamic and creative workplace.

Encouraging Experimentation and Risk-Taking

Creativity thrives in an environment where experimentation and risk-taking are encouraged. Encourage employees to explore new ideas, try out different approaches, and learn from their mistakes. Create a culture where failure is viewed as a learning opportunity rather than a setback. This mindset can help reduce the fear of failure and encourage employees to take risks and think creatively.

One way to promote experimentation is by allocating time for innovation. For example, you could implement a "20% time" policy, where employees are allowed to spend a portion of their workweek on projects of their choosing. This can lead to new ideas and innovations that benefit the organisation. Additionally, consider organising hackathons, workshops, and creative challenges to stimulate creative thinking and collaboration.

Recognise and reward creative efforts, even if they don't result in immediate success. Celebrating the process of innovation can reinforce the importance of creativity and encourage employees to continue experimenting. By fostering a culture that values and supports risk-taking, you can unleash the creative potential of your team and drive continuous improvement.

Providing Resources and Tools

Access to the right resources and tools is crucial for fostering creativity. Ensure that employees have the materials, technology, and support they need to bring their ideas to life. This could include providing high-quality software, access to online courses, and a well-stocked office supply closet. Investing in these resources demonstrates your commitment to supporting creativity and innovation.

Offer training and development opportunities to help employees enhance their creative skills. This could include workshops on creative thinking, design thinking, or problem-solving techniques. Encouraging employees to attend conferences and industry events can also expose them to new ideas and trends. By investing in your team's professional development, you can equip them with the skills and knowledge they need to innovate and excel.

Create an environment that inspires creativity by designing a visually stimulating workspace. Use colours, artwork, and natural elements to create an inviting and energising atmosphere. Ensure that the workspace is comfortable and conducive to creative thinking, with ample natural light, ergonomic furniture, and quiet areas for focused work. By providing a supportive and inspiring environment, you can enhance your team's creativity and productivity.

Promoting Collaboration

Collaboration is a key driver of creativity. When employees work together, they can share ideas, challenge each other's thinking, and develop innovative solutions. Encourage collaboration by creating opportunities for team members to work together on projects and initiatives. This can be achieved through cross-functional teams, brainstorming sessions, and collaborative workspaces.

Foster a culture of collaboration by recognising and celebrating team achievements. Highlight the value of diverse perspectives and the importance of working together to achieve common goals. Provide opportunities for team-building activities, such as workshops, social events, and retreats, to strengthen relationships and build trust among team members. A strong sense of camaraderie can enhance communication and collaboration, leading to more creative outcomes.

Leverage digital collaboration tools to facilitate teamwork, especially if your team includes remote workers. Platforms such as Slack, Microsoft Teams, and Trello can help streamline communication and project management. These tools allow team members to share ideas, provide feedback, and track progress in real-time, making it easier to collaborate effectively. By promoting collaboration, you can harness the collective creativity of your team and drive innovation.

Recognising and Rewarding Creativity

Recognising and rewarding creativity is essential for maintaining a creative work environment. Acknowledge and celebrate creative efforts and achievements, both big and small. This can be done through formal recognition programmes, such as "Employee of the Month" awards, or informal gestures, such as public praise during team meetings. By valuing and rewarding creativity, you can motivate employees to continue thinking innovatively.

Consider implementing a reward system that incentivises creative contributions. This could include bonuses, additional time off, or opportunities for professional development. Tailor the rewards to suit the preferences and interests of your team members. By offering meaningful incentives, you can encourage employees to invest time and effort into creative thinking and problem-solving.

Create a culture of recognition where employees are encouraged to acknowledge each other's creative contributions. This can be facilitated through peer recognition programmes, where team members can nominate each other for creative achievements. By fostering a supportive and appreciative environment, you can reinforce the importance of creativity and inspire your team to strive for continuous innovation.

Encouraging Continuous Learning

Continuous learning is essential for maintaining a creative and innovative workforce. Encourage employees to seek out new knowledge and skills through various learning opportunities. This could include attending workshops, enrolling in online courses, or participating in industry conferences. Providing access to resources such as books, articles, and podcasts can also support continuous learning.

Create a culture that values and prioritises learning by offering regular training and development programmes. Encourage employees to share their knowledge and experiences with the team through presentations, lunch-and-learn sessions, or mentoring programmes. This collaborative approach to learning can foster a culture of curiosity and open-mindedness, which are key drivers of creativity.

Support learning by providing time and space for employees to explore new ideas and experiment with different approaches. This could include offering dedicated innovation time or creating a library or quiet area for focused learning. By prioritising continuous learning, you can keep your team's skills and knowledge up-to-date, ensuring they remain agile and capable of adapting to new challenges and opportunities.

Creating a Safe Space for Creativity

A safe space for creativity is one where employees feel comfortable taking risks and expressing their ideas without fear of judgement or criticism. Create this environment by promoting psychological safety, where team members trust that they can share their thoughts and opinions openly. This can be achieved by modelling inclusive and respectful behaviour, actively listening to employees, and addressing any negative behaviours or attitudes.

Encourage a culture of experimentation and learning from mistakes. Emphasise that failure is a natural part of the creative process and an opportunity for growth and improvement. Share stories of past failures and the lessons learned from them to normalise the experience and reduce the stigma associated with making mistakes. By creating a safe space for creativity, you can empower employees to take risks and explore new ideas.

Provide regular opportunities for employees to share their ideas and receive feedback in a supportive and constructive manner. This could include brainstorming sessions, innovation forums, or one-on-one meetings. Ensure that feedback is specific, actionable, and focused on improvement rather than criticism. By fostering a safe and supportive environment, you can encourage employees to think creatively and contribute their best ideas.

Embracing Diversity and Inclusion

Diversity and inclusion are critical components of a creative work environment. A diverse team brings together different perspectives, experiences, and ideas, which can lead to more innovative solutions. Embrace diversity by actively seeking to hire and retain employees from various backgrounds, cultures, and disciplines. Ensure that your recruitment and retention practices are inclusive and free from bias.

Promote an inclusive culture by valuing and respecting the unique contributions of each team member. Encourage open dialogue and provide opportunities for employees to share their experiences and perspectives. Foster a sense of belonging by celebrating cultural diversity and creating an environment where everyone feels valued and included. By embracing diversity and inclusion, you can enhance creativity and drive innovation.

Support diversity and inclusion through training and development programmes that raise awareness and build skills in cultural competence, unconscious bias, and inclusive leadership. Encourage employees to engage in open and honest conversations about diversity and inclusion and to actively seek out and consider diverse perspectives in their work. By creating a diverse and inclusive workplace, you can unlock the full creative potential of your team.

Fostering a creative environment at work requires intentional efforts to promote open communication, flexibility, experimentation, collaboration, and continuous learning. By recognising and rewarding creativity, creating a safe and inclusive space, and providing the necessary resources and tools, you can unlock the full potential of your team. Embrace these strategies to create a dynamic and innovative workplace that drives success and personal fulfilment for all employees.

20

Innovative Thinking for Career Advancement

Innovative thinking is a powerful tool that can propel your career to new heights. By approaching your professional development with creativity and open-mindedness, you can unlock opportunities, solve problems more effectively, and stand out in your field. In this chapter, we will explore various strategies for using innovative thinking to advance your career, helping you achieve greater success and fulfilment.

Embracing a Growth Mindset

A growth mindset is the belief that your abilities and intelligence can be developed through dedication and hard work. Embracing this mindset is essential for fostering innovative thinking. When you view challenges as opportunities to learn and grow, you are more likely to take risks, experiment with new ideas, and persist in the face of setbacks.

To cultivate a growth mindset, start by reframing your perspective on failure. Instead of seeing it as a negative outcome, view it as a valuable learning experience that can provide insights and drive improvement. Celebrate your efforts and progress, rather than focusing solely on outcomes. This approach encourages continuous learning and development, which are crucial for career advancement.

Additionally, seek feedback regularly and use it constructively. Feedback provides an external perspective on your performance and can highlight areas for improvement that you might not have noticed. By actively seeking and applying feedback, you demonstrate a commitment to growth and a willingness to adapt and innovate.

Leveraging Creativity in Problem-Solving

Effective problem-solving is a critical skill for career advancement, and creativity plays a significant role in developing innovative solutions. Instead of relying on traditional methods, use creative thinking techniques to approach problems from different angles. Techniques such as brainstorming, mind mapping, and the SCAMPER method can help generate a wide range of potential solutions.

When faced with a problem, take the time to understand it fully before jumping to conclusions. Break the problem down into smaller components and explore each one in detail. This analytical approach, combined with creative thinking, can lead to more effective and innovative solutions. Encourage input from colleagues and collaborate on finding solutions, as diverse perspectives can spark new ideas.

Document your problem-solving process and outcomes. This not only helps you track your progress but also provides a valuable resource for future reference. Sharing your innovative solutions with your team or management can demonstrate your problem-solving abilities and contribute to your professional reputation.

Seeking Continuous Learning Opportunities

In today's rapidly changing job market, continuous learning is essential for staying relevant and competitive. Innovative thinkers actively seek opportunities to expand their knowledge and skills. This could include enrolling in online courses, attending workshops and conferences, or reading industry-related books and articles.

Identify areas where you can improve or where new skills could enhance your career prospects. Set learning goals and create a plan to achieve them. This proactive approach to personal development shows initiative and a commitment to your career growth. Additionally, staying updated with the latest trends and technologies in your field can position you as a forward-thinking professional.

Networking is another valuable learning tool. Engage with industry peers, join professional associations, and participate in online forums and communities. Networking can provide insights, resources, and mentorship opportunities that support your continuous learning journey. By connecting with others, you can gain new perspectives and stay informed about industry developments.

Innovating Within Your Current Role

You don't need a new job to apply innovative thinking; you can start by making improvements within your current role. Look for inefficiencies, outdated processes, or unmet needs and propose creative solutions. This proactive approach not only enhances your productivity but also demonstrates your value to your organisation.

Identify key areas where you can make a difference. For instance, you might streamline a workflow, introduce a new technology, or develop a more effective communication strategy. Present your ideas to your manager with a clear plan and potential benefits. By taking the initiative to innovate, you show leadership qualities and a commitment to continuous improvement.

Document your achievements and the impact of your innovations. This record can be invaluable during performance reviews or when seeking promotions. Highlighting your contributions demonstrates your ability to think creatively and deliver tangible results, making you a strong candidate for career advancement.

Building a Personal Brand

Building a strong personal brand is crucial for career advancement, and innovative thinking can help you stand out in a crowded marketplace. Your personal brand reflects your unique skills, experiences, and values. By presenting yourself creatively, you can attract new opportunities and establish yourself as a thought leader in your field.

Start by identifying your unique strengths and what sets you apart from others. Develop a clear message that communicates your expertise and value. Use various platforms, such as social media, professional networking sites, and personal websites, to showcase your skills and accomplishments. Consistently sharing valuable content and engaging with your audience can help build your reputation and credibility.

Networking also plays a key role in building your personal brand. Attend industry events, participate in online discussions, and seek out speaking opportunities. Building relationships with influential people in your field can open doors to new opportunities and further establish your personal brand. By leveraging innovative thinking in your branding efforts, you can create a lasting and impactful presence in your industry.

Embracing Technology and Innovation

Staying ahead of technological advancements is crucial for career growth in today's digital age. Embracing new technologies and innovations can enhance your productivity, efficiency, and competitiveness. Stay informed about emerging technologies relevant to your field and explore how they can be applied to improve your work processes.

Experiment with new tools and software that can streamline your tasks and boost your efficiency. For example, project management tools, automation software, and data analytics platforms can help you work smarter and more effectively. By integrating technology into your daily routine, you can free up time for more strategic and creative activities.

Continuously seek opportunities to innovate by leveraging technology. Propose technology-driven solutions to address challenges or improve outcomes within your organisation. Demonstrating your ability to adapt to and leverage new technologies can position you as a forward-thinking professional and enhance your career prospects.

Cultivating a Network of Innovators

Surrounding yourself with innovative thinkers can inspire and motivate you to develop your own creative thinking skills. Cultivate a network of individuals who share your passion for innovation and career advancement. These connections can provide valuable insights, support, and collaboration opportunities.

Join professional associations, attend industry events, and participate in online forums to connect with like-minded professionals. Engage in meaningful conversations, share ideas, and collaborate on projects. Building strong relationships with innovative thinkers can create a supportive community that encourages continuous growth and development.

Seek mentorship from individuals who have successfully leveraged innovative thinking in their careers. A mentor can provide guidance, share their experiences, and offer valuable advice. By learning from those who have achieved success through innovation, you can gain insights and strategies to apply to your own career advancement.

Balancing Innovation with Practicality

While innovative thinking is essential, it's important to balance creativity with practicality. Innovative ideas need to be feasible and aligned with organisational goals to be implemented successfully. When proposing innovative solutions, consider the resources, time, and potential impact on your organisation.

Conduct thorough research and analysis to support your ideas. Develop a clear plan that outlines the steps needed to implement your solution, including potential challenges and how to address them. Present your ideas with a focus on the benefits and how they align with organisational objectives. By balancing innovation with practicality, you can increase the likelihood of your ideas being accepted and implemented.

Regularly review and refine your innovative strategies to ensure they remain relevant and effective. Stay open to feedback and be willing to make adjustments as needed. This iterative approach allows you to continuously improve and adapt your innovations, ensuring they deliver the desired results and support your career advancement.

Innovative thinking is a powerful catalyst for career advancement. By embracing a growth mindset, leveraging creativity in problem-solving, seeking continuous learning opportunities, innovating within your current role, building a personal brand, embracing technology, cultivating a network of innovators, and balancing innovation with practicality, you can unlock new opportunities and achieve greater success in your career. Incorporate these strategies into your professional journey and watch as your creativity and innovative thinking propel you towards new heights of achievement and fulfilment.

21

Finding and Following Your Passion

Finding and following your passion can lead to a more fulfilling and successful life. When you pursue what you love, work feels less like a chore and more like a rewarding journey. However, discovering your passion and turning it into a reality can be challenging. In this chapter, we will explore strategies to help you identify your passion and practical steps to follow it, enabling you to lead a more meaningful and inspired life.

Understanding Passion

Passion is an intense enthusiasm or desire for something. It drives you to pursue activities with dedication and joy. Finding your passion is about discovering what truly excites and motivates you, what you can lose yourself in for hours without noticing the time pass. Understanding passion begins with self-reflection and exploration.

Reflect on activities and experiences that have brought you joy and satisfaction in the past. Think about hobbies, projects, or subjects that capture your interest and make you feel energised. Ask yourself what you would do if money and time were no object. These reflections can provide valuable clues about your passions and help you identify patterns in what you enjoy.

It's important to recognise that passions can evolve over time. What excites you today may change in the future, and that's perfectly normal. Be open to exploring new interests and allowing your passions to develop naturally. By staying curious and adaptable, you can continuously discover and refine what truly drives you.

Exploring Your Interests

Exploring your interests is a key step in finding your passion. Take time to try out new activities and experiences. Sign up for workshops, join clubs, or take classes in subjects that intrigue you. This hands-on exploration can help you identify what you enjoy and what resonates with you on a deeper level.

Don't be afraid to step outside your comfort zone and experiment with different activities. Sometimes, passions are discovered in unexpected places. Volunteering, travelling, and meeting new people can also expose you to new interests and perspectives. The more you explore, the better you can understand what excites and motivates you.

Keep a journal to document your experiences and reflections. Write down what you enjoyed, what you didn't, and any insights you gained. Over time, this journal can reveal patterns and help you identify recurring themes in your interests. By actively exploring and reflecting on your experiences, you can move closer to finding your passion.

Identifying Your Strengths

Your strengths are closely linked to your passions. When you engage in activities that align with your natural talents, you are more likely to feel fulfilled and motivated. Identifying your strengths involves understanding what you are good at and what comes naturally to you.

Take stock of your skills and abilities. Reflect on past achievements and consider the tasks you excel at and enjoy. Seek feedback from friends, family, and colleagues to gain an external perspective on your strengths. This can provide valuable insights and help you recognise talents you might overlook.

Once you have identified your strengths, think about how they can be applied to different activities and careers. Look for intersections between your skills and your interests. By aligning your strengths with your passions, you can find a path that is both fulfilling and rewarding. Embracing your strengths can also boost your confidence and drive you to pursue your passion with greater enthusiasm.

Overcoming Fear and Doubt

Fear and doubt can be significant obstacles when trying to find and follow your passion. It's natural to worry about failure, judgment, or the unknown. However, allowing these fears to hold you back can prevent you from discovering and pursuing what truly excites you.

Address your fears by breaking them down and challenging them. Identify the specific concerns that are holding you back and consider how realistic they are. Often, our fears are exaggerated or based on assumptions rather than facts. By questioning and reframing your fears, you can reduce their power over you.

Take small, manageable steps towards your passion. This gradual approach can help build your confidence and reduce anxiety. Celebrate your progress, no matter how small, and use it as motivation to keep moving forward. Surround yourself with supportive people who encourage and believe in you. Their support can boost your confidence and help you stay focused on your goals.

Setting Clear Goals

Setting clear goals is essential for turning your passion into reality. Goals provide direction and a sense of purpose, helping you stay focused and motivated. When setting goals, make them specific, measurable, achievable, relevant, and time-bound (SMART).

Start by defining your long-term vision. What do you ultimately want to achieve with your passion? Break this vision down into smaller, actionable steps. Set short-term and medium-term goals that guide you towards your long-term objective. This step-by-step approach makes your journey more manageable and less overwhelming.

Regularly review and adjust your goals as needed. As you progress, you may discover new interests or opportunities that require you to adapt your plan. Stay flexible and open to change, but remain committed to your overall vision. By setting and pursuing clear goals, you can steadily advance towards making your passion a central part of your life.

Balancing Passion and Practicality

While it's important to follow your passion, it's also essential to balance it with practicality. Consider how you can realistically integrate your passion into your life and career. This might involve making compromises or finding creative solutions to balance your personal and professional responsibilities.

Evaluate the financial implications of pursuing your passion. If your passion doesn't initially provide financial stability, consider how you can support yourself while working towards your goals. This might involve maintaining a part-time job, freelancing, or finding ways to monetise your passion gradually.

Seek advice and mentorship from individuals who have successfully integrated their passions into their careers. Their experiences can provide valuable insights and guidance. By balancing passion with practicality, you can create a sustainable and fulfilling path that allows you to pursue what you love without compromising your financial stability.

Staying Persistent and Resilient

Pursuing your passion requires persistence and resilience. Challenges and setbacks are inevitable, but they should not deter you from your path. Stay committed to your goals and maintain a positive attitude, even when faced with obstacles.

Develop strategies to cope with setbacks and maintain your motivation. This might involve setting aside time for self-care, practising mindfulness, or seeking support from your network. Reflect on your progress regularly and celebrate your achievements, no matter how small. This can boost your confidence and keep you focused on your long-term vision.

Remember that success is a journey, not a destination. Embrace the process of learning, growing, and evolving as you pursue your passion. Stay flexible and open to new opportunities, and don't be afraid to adjust your path as needed. By staying persistent and resilient, you can overcome challenges and continue moving towards a fulfilling and passionate life.

Turning Passion into a Career

Turning your passion into a career is a rewarding but often challenging endeavour. Start by identifying ways to monetise your passion. This might involve offering services, creating products, or sharing your expertise through teaching or consulting. Research the market and identify opportunities where your passion and skills can meet a demand.

Develop a business plan that outlines your goals, target audience, and strategies for growth. This plan can guide your efforts and provide a roadmap for success. Seek advice from professionals or mentors who can offer insights and help you refine your approach. Networking with others in your field can also provide valuable connections and opportunities.

Be prepared for a period of transition as you work to turn your passion into a career. This might involve balancing a part-time job with your passion projects or gradually building your client base. Stay focused on your long-term vision and be patient with the process. By persistently working towards your goals, you can eventually create a career that aligns with your passion and provides both personal and financial fulfilment.

Finding and following your passion can lead to a more meaningful and successful life. By understanding your passions, exploring your interests, identifying your strengths, and overcoming fear and doubt, you can discover what truly excites you. Setting clear goals, balancing passion with practicality, building a support network, and staying persistent and resilient are essential steps in turning your passion into reality. Embrace this journey with an open heart and mind, and let your passion guide you towards a fulfilling and inspired life.

22

Building Resilience and Staying Motivated

Resilience and motivation are crucial for achieving long-term success and maintaining a positive outlook in the face of challenges. Developing these qualities can help you navigate difficulties, stay focused on your goals, and keep moving forward. In this chapter, we will explore strategies for building resilience and staying motivated, helping you cultivate a strong and determined mindset for achieving your dreams.

Understanding Resilience

Resilience is the ability to bounce back from setbacks, adapt to change, and keep going despite difficulties. It's not about avoiding challenges but about facing them head-on and emerging stronger. Understanding resilience begins with recognising that setbacks are a natural part of life and that growth often comes from overcoming adversity.

To build resilience, start by shifting your perspective on challenges. Instead of viewing them as insurmountable obstacles, see them as opportunities for growth and learning. This mindset can help you stay positive and proactive when faced with difficulties. Remember that every setback is a chance to develop new skills, gain insights, and build strength.

Cultivate a growth mindset, where you believe that your abilities and intelligence can be developed through effort and perseverance. Embrace challenges as a way to stretch your capabilities and improve. This mindset fosters resilience by encouraging you to see setbacks as temporary and manageable, rather than permanent and overwhelming.

Building Emotional Strength

Emotional strength is a key component of resilience. It involves managing your emotions effectively, staying calm under pressure, and maintaining a positive outlook. Building emotional strength requires self-awareness and emotional regulation skills.

Practice mindfulness to increase your emotional awareness. Mindfulness involves paying attention to the present moment without judgment. It can help you recognise your emotions as they arise and respond to them more thoughtfully. Regular mindfulness practice, such as meditation or deep-breathing exercises, can improve your emotional regulation and reduce stress.

Develop coping strategies for dealing with negative emotions. This might include journaling, talking to a trusted friend, or engaging in activities that bring you joy and relaxation. Having a toolbox of coping mechanisms can help you navigate difficult emotions and maintain your resilience. By building emotional strength, you can stay grounded and focused, even in challenging situations.

Setting Realistic Goals

Setting realistic goals is essential for staying motivated and maintaining resilience. Clear, achievable goals provide direction and a sense of purpose, making it easier to stay focused and committed. Break down larger goals into smaller, manageable steps to avoid feeling overwhelmed and to track your progress more effectively.

When setting goals, ensure they are specific, measurable, achievable, relevant, and time-bound (SMART). This framework helps you create clear and actionable objectives. For example, instead of setting a vague goal like "get fit," set a specific goal such as "exercise for 30 minutes three times a week." This clarity makes it easier to stay motivated and measure your progress.

Regularly review and adjust your goals as needed. Life is dynamic, and your goals may need to evolve with changing circumstances. Stay flexible and open to revising your plans to stay aligned with your overall vision. By setting and pursuing realistic goals, you can maintain a sense of achievement and motivation, even in the face of setbacks.

Finding Inspiration and Purpose

Finding inspiration and a sense of purpose can significantly boost your motivation. When you have a clear understanding of why you are pursuing your goals, it becomes easier to stay focused and driven. Take time to reflect on what truly matters to you and what you want to achieve in life.

Identify role models and sources of inspiration. This could be people who have achieved similar goals, books, quotes, or personal experiences that resonate with you. Surround yourself with positive influences that remind you of your purpose and inspire you to keep going. Engaging with inspiring content can rekindle your motivation and help you stay committed to your goals.

Consider your values and how they align with your goals. Understanding the deeper meaning behind your aspirations can provide a strong sense of purpose. For example, if one of your goals is to advance in your career, think about how achieving this will impact your personal growth, financial stability, and ability to contribute to your community. By connecting your goals to your values, you can create a powerful source of motivation that sustains you through challenges.

Maintaining a Positive Mindset

A positive mindset is essential for building resilience and staying motivated. Optimism and positive thinking can help you see opportunities where others see obstacles and keep you focused on solutions rather than problems. Developing a positive mindset involves practising gratitude, reframing negative thoughts, and surrounding yourself with positivity.

Start a gratitude journal to regularly reflect on the positive aspects of your life. Each day, write down three things you are grateful for. This practice can shift your focus from what's lacking to what's abundant in your life, fostering a more positive outlook. Gratitude can enhance your resilience by helping you appreciate the good, even during tough times.

Reframe negative thoughts by challenging their validity and considering alternative perspectives. Instead of thinking, "I can't do this," try, "This is challenging, but I can learn and improve." This shift in thinking can reduce feelings of helplessness and boost your confidence. Surround yourself with positive influences, such as supportive friends, uplifting content, and inspiring environments, to reinforce your positive mindset.

Practising Self-Care

Self-care is crucial for maintaining resilience and motivation. Taking care of your physical, mental, and emotional well-being ensures you have the energy and strength to pursue your goals. Self-care involves engaging in activities that promote relaxation, joy, and overall health.

Prioritise physical health by maintaining a balanced diet, exercising regularly, and getting adequate sleep. Physical well-being directly impacts your energy levels, mood, and ability to handle stress. Incorporate regular physical activity into your routine, whether it's a daily walk, yoga, or a gym session. Proper nutrition and rest are also essential for optimal functioning and resilience.

Mental and emotional self-care involves activities that reduce stress and promote well-being. This could include practising mindfulness, engaging in hobbies you enjoy, or spending time with loved ones. Make time for relaxation and leisure activities that rejuvenate you. Setting boundaries to protect your time and energy is also an important aspect of self-care. By prioritising self-care, you can maintain the resilience and motivation needed to achieve your goals.

Embracing Flexibility and Adaptability

Flexibility and adaptability are key traits of resilient individuals. The ability to adapt to changing circumstances and remain open to new possibilities can help you navigate challenges and stay motivated. Embrace change as a natural part of life and be willing to adjust your plans as needed.

Develop a flexible mindset by practising problem-solving and creative thinking. When faced with unexpected changes, look for alternative solutions and opportunities. This proactive approach can help you stay resilient and maintain your motivation, even when things don't go as planned. Being adaptable means being open to learning and growth, which are essential for long-term success.

Accept that setbacks and changes are inevitable. Instead of resisting or fearing change, view it as an opportunity to learn and grow. Stay curious and open to new experiences, and be willing to revise your goals and strategies as needed. By embracing flexibility and adaptability, you can maintain a positive outlook and continue moving forward, no matter what challenges arise.

Celebrating Progress and Achievements

Celebrating your progress and achievements is vital for maintaining motivation. Recognising and rewarding yourself for your efforts can boost your confidence and reinforce your commitment to your goals. Make it a habit to acknowledge both big and small milestones on your journey.

Set up a reward system to celebrate your achievements. This could involve treating yourself to something you enjoy, taking a break, or sharing your success with loved ones. Celebrating your progress reminds you of how far you've come and provides motivation to keep going. It also helps to build a positive association with the effort and dedication you invest in your goals.

Reflect on your accomplishments regularly. Take time to review what you have achieved and the progress you have made towards your goals. This reflection can provide a sense of satisfaction and reinforce your motivation. By celebrating your successes, you create positive reinforcement that encourages you to continue striving for your aspirations.

Building resilience and staying motivated are essential for achieving long-term success and personal fulfilment. By understanding and developing resilience, building emotional strength, setting realistic goals, finding inspiration and purpose, maintaining a positive mindset, practising self-care, embracing flexibility, and celebrating progress, you can cultivate a strong and determined mindset. Embrace these strategies to navigate challenges, stay focused on your goals, and lead a fulfilling and inspired life.

23

Case Studies

Case Study: Know Your Mind

In the journey towards creative success, understanding one's own mind is a crucial step. Knowing your mind involves recognising your strengths, acknowledging your weaknesses, and understanding how you think and process information. This self-awareness can unlock your creative potential and pave the way for personal and professional growth. Let's explore a case study that highlights the importance of knowing your mind and how it can lead to remarkable success.

Background

Meet Sarah, a talented graphic designer in her late twenties working for a well-known marketing agency. Despite her impressive portfolio and the admiration of her peers, Sarah often felt stuck in her career. She was constantly battling self-doubt and felt she wasn't living up to her creative potential. Her projects, while competent, lacked the spark that would set them apart in a competitive industry. Sarah knew she needed a change but didn't know where to start.

The Realisation

Sarah's turning point came during a team-building workshop her company organised. The workshop focused on self-awareness and included various exercises to help participants understand their thinking patterns, strengths, and areas for improvement. One of the exercises was a detailed personality assessment, which provided insights into how each participant processed information and approached problem-solving.

Sarah discovered that she was a natural visual thinker, excelling in conceptualising ideas through images and visual metaphors. However, she also learned that she had a tendency to overthink and second-guess her ideas, which led to creative blocks. This realisation was eye-opening for Sarah. She understood that her self-doubt stemmed from a lack of confidence in her natural thinking style.

Embracing Strengths

Armed with this new knowledge, Sarah decided to embrace her visual thinking strengths. She started incorporating more visual brainstorming techniques into her workflow. Instead of relying solely on lists and written plans, she used mind maps, sketching, and mood boards to capture her ideas. This approach not only played to her strengths but also made the creative process more enjoyable and less stressful.

Sarah's newfound confidence in her thinking style began to reflect in her work. Her designs became more innovative and visually striking. She felt more connected to her projects and noticed that her ideas flowed more freely. By understanding and embracing her natural way of thinking, Sarah unlocked a new level of creativity that had been dormant for years.

Addressing Weaknesses

While Sarah was thriving by leveraging her strengths, she knew it was equally important to address her weaknesses. The personality assessment had revealed that her tendency to overthink was holding her back. To combat this, Sarah implemented a few strategies to manage her overthinking.

First, she set time limits for brainstorming sessions. This forced her to generate ideas quickly without overanalysing them. She also adopted a more iterative approach to her work, allowing herself to make revisions and improvements along the way rather than striving for perfection from the start. Additionally, Sarah sought feedback from colleagues earlier in the process, which helped her gain different perspectives and reduce the pressure she put on herself.

These changes made a significant difference. Sarah found that by setting boundaries on her thinking time and embracing an iterative process, she was able to produce more creative and refined work. Her confidence grew as she saw the positive impact of these strategies on her productivity and creativity.

Leveraging Self-Awareness for Career Growth

With her enhanced self-awareness, Sarah decided to take her career to the next level. She set new goals that aligned with her strengths and interests. One of her ambitions was to become a lead designer for major marketing campaigns, a role that required both creative vision and leadership skills.

To achieve this, Sarah knew she needed to develop her leadership abilities. She enrolled in a leadership training programme that focused on communication, team management, and strategic thinking. The training helped her understand how to leverage her strengths as a visual thinker to inspire and guide her team. She learned to communicate her ideas more effectively and to create an environment where her team felt encouraged to share their own creative insights.

Sarah's efforts paid off. Her newfound confidence and leadership skills caught the attention of her superiors, and she was soon promoted to lead designer. In her new role, Sarah continued to use her self-awareness to drive success. She implemented collaborative brainstorming sessions, visual planning techniques, and regular feedback loops within her team. These practices not only improved the quality of the team's work but also fostered a more creative and supportive work environment.

Overcoming Challenges

Despite her progress, Sarah faced challenges along the way. One major challenge was the pressure of leading high-stakes projects and meeting tight deadlines. At times, the stress threatened to trigger her old habits of overthinking and self-doubt. However, Sarah's commitment to self-awareness helped her navigate these challenges.

She maintained her practice of setting time limits for brainstorming and focused on the iterative process. Additionally, she prioritised self-care to manage stress. Regular exercise, mindfulness meditation, and hobbies outside of work helped her stay balanced and resilient. By taking care of her mental and physical well-being, Sarah was better equipped to handle the demands of her role and continue delivering high-quality work.

The Impact of Knowing Your Mind

Sarah's journey illustrates the profound impact of knowing your mind. By understanding her strengths and weaknesses, she was able to unlock her creative potential and achieve remarkable success. Her self-awareness allowed her to develop strategies that played to her strengths and addressed her challenges, leading to personal and professional growth.

Sarah's story also highlights the importance of continuous learning and adaptation. As she progressed in her career, she remained open to new insights and willing to refine her strategies. This mindset enabled her to stay resilient in the face of challenges and to continuously improve her skills and creativity.

Lessons Learned

Sarah's case study offers valuable lessons for anyone seeking to enhance their creative mind and achieve success:

1. **Self-Awareness is Key**: Understanding your thinking patterns, strengths, and weaknesses is the foundation of personal and professional growth. Use tools like personality assessments and self-reflection to gain insights into your mind.
2. **Embrace Your Strengths**: Leverage your natural abilities and thinking styles to enhance your creativity and productivity. Find ways to incorporate your strengths into your daily work and projects.
3. **Address Your Weaknesses**: Identify areas where you struggle and develop strategies to manage them. This might involve setting boundaries, seeking feedback, or adopting new approaches.
4. **Continuous Learning and Adaptation**: Stay open to new insights and be willing to refine your strategies as you progress. Continuous learning and adaptation are essential for long-term success.
5. **Balance and Self-Care**: Managing stress and maintaining balance are crucial for sustaining creativity and productivity. Prioritise self-care and find activities that help you stay grounded and resilient.

Conclusion

Knowing your mind is a powerful tool for unlocking your creative potential and achieving success. Sarah's journey demonstrates how self-awareness can transform your approach to work and life, leading to greater fulfilment and accomplishments. By understanding your strengths, addressing your weaknesses, and continuously learning and adapting, you can navigate challenges and reach new heights in your personal and professional endeavours. Embrace the journey of self-discovery and let your creative mind guide you towards a successful and inspired life.

Case Study: Unleashing Creativity

Creativity is a powerful force that drives innovation, problem-solving, and personal expression. It can transform ordinary ideas into extraordinary achievements and plays a vital role in personal and professional success. In this chapter, we will explore a case study that highlights the transformative power of creativity and the journey of an individual who used creativity to overcome challenges and achieve remarkable success.

Background

Meet James, a young entrepreneur in his early thirties with a passion for technology and innovation. James founded a small tech startup that specialised in developing software solutions for small businesses. Despite his technical skills and dedication, James found it challenging to differentiate his company in a highly competitive market. His initial projects, while functional, lacked the innovative edge needed to capture the attention of potential clients and investors.

The Realisation

James's turning point came when he attended a tech conference where he was inspired by a keynote speaker who emphasised the importance of creativity in technology and business. The speaker shared stories of how creative thinking led to groundbreaking innovations and business success. This struck a chord with James, who realised that while he was technically proficient, he had not been leveraging creativity to its full potential.

Determined to change his approach, James began researching ways to foster creativity within himself and his team. He read books on creative thinking, attended workshops, and sought advice from mentors who had successfully integrated creativity into their work. James was particularly intrigued by the concept of design thinking, a creative problem-solving process that involves empathy, ideation, and experimentation.

Implementing Design Thinking

James decided to implement design thinking in his startup. He introduced his team to the process, which begins with understanding the user's needs through empathy. This involved conducting interviews and surveys with small business owners to gain insights into their pain points and challenges. By putting himself in the users' shoes, James was able to identify unmet needs that his software could address.

The next step was ideation, where James and his team brainstormed a wide range of ideas to solve the identified problems. They encouraged wild ideas and suspended judgment to foster a free-flowing creative environment. The team used techniques such as mind mapping and sketching to visualise their ideas. This collaborative approach not only generated a wealth of innovative concepts but also boosted team morale and engagement.

The final step was prototyping and testing. James and his team developed quick, low-cost prototypes of their best ideas and tested them with real users. This iterative process allowed them to gather feedback, refine their solutions, and identify the most promising concepts. By embracing design thinking, James's startup was able to develop innovative software solutions that stood out in the market.

Embracing a Creative Culture

Inspired by the success of design thinking, James decided to cultivate a creative culture within his startup. He believed that fostering an environment that encouraged creativity would lead to continuous innovation and long-term success. To achieve this, James implemented several key strategies.

First, he encouraged open communication and collaboration. James established regular brainstorming sessions and open forums where team members could share their ideas and provide feedback. He also promoted a flat organisational structure, where everyone's input was valued regardless of their position. This inclusive approach helped to create a supportive and creative atmosphere.

Second, James provided resources and opportunities for creative development. He allocated time and budget for team members to attend workshops, conferences, and online courses focused on creativity and innovation. He also introduced "innovation days," where employees could work on passion projects or explore new ideas unrelated to their regular tasks. This not only sparked creativity but also fostered a sense of ownership and motivation among the team.

Lastly, James recognised and celebrated creative efforts. He implemented a reward system that acknowledged innovative ideas and successful projects. Whether it was through public recognition, bonuses, or additional time off, James ensured that creativity was rewarded and appreciated. This reinforced the importance of creativity and motivated the team to continue thinking outside the box.

Overcoming Challenges

Despite the positive changes, James faced challenges along the way. One significant obstacle was the initial resistance to change. Some team members were sceptical about the emphasis on creativity and design thinking, fearing it would distract from their technical work. To address this, James led by example and demonstrated the tangible benefits of creative thinking through successful projects and client feedback.

Another challenge was balancing creativity with practicality. While generating innovative ideas was exciting, it was crucial to ensure they were feasible and aligned with the company's goals. James and his team developed a framework for evaluating ideas based on their potential impact, feasibility, and alignment with user needs. This helped to prioritise and refine the best concepts, ensuring that creativity translated into practical solutions.

Maintaining momentum was also a challenge. The initial enthusiasm for creativity could wane over time, especially when faced with tight deadlines and routine tasks. To keep the creative spirit alive, James continuously reinforced the importance of creativity through regular workshops, team-building activities, and inspirational talks. He also encouraged a culture of continuous learning and curiosity, reminding the team that creativity was a journey, not a destination.

Achieving Success

James's commitment to fostering creativity paid off. His startup began to attract attention for its innovative software solutions that addressed real user needs in unique and effective ways. The company's reputation grew, leading to increased client interest and investment opportunities. James's creative approach not only differentiated his startup in the market but also drove its growth and success.

One of the standout projects was a user-friendly accounting software tailored for small businesses. By applying design thinking, James's team developed an intuitive interface that simplified complex accounting tasks. The software received rave reviews from users and quickly became a best-seller, significantly boosting the company's revenue and market presence.

James also noticed a positive shift in the company culture. Team members were more engaged, motivated, and willing to share their ideas. The collaborative and supportive environment led to higher job satisfaction and lower turnover rates. The culture of creativity not only drove innovation but also created a more cohesive and resilient team.

The Impact of Creativity

James's journey highlights the transformative power of creativity in achieving success. By embracing creative thinking and fostering a creative culture, he was able to overcome challenges, differentiate his startup, and achieve remarkable growth. His story demonstrates that creativity is not limited to artistic pursuits but is a valuable asset in any field.

Creativity drives innovation by encouraging new ways of thinking and solving problems. It enables individuals and organisations to adapt to changing environments and stay ahead of the competition. By fostering creativity, you can unlock new opportunities, improve processes, and deliver exceptional value to your clients and stakeholders.

Furthermore, creativity enhances personal and professional fulfilment. Engaging in creative activities and thinking can boost motivation, reduce stress, and increase overall job satisfaction. It fosters a sense of purpose and achievement, contributing to a more balanced and fulfilling life.

Lessons Learned

James's case study offers valuable lessons for anyone seeking to harness the power of creativity:

1. **Embrace Creative Processes**: Implement structured creative processes, such as design thinking, to foster innovation and solve problems effectively. These processes provide a framework for generating, refining, and implementing creative ideas.
2. **Foster a Creative Culture**: Create an environment that encourages open communication, collaboration, and continuous learning. Provide resources and opportunities for creative development and recognise creative efforts to motivate and inspire your team.
3. **Balance Creativity with Practicality**: Ensure that creative ideas are feasible and aligned with organisational goals. Develop a framework for evaluating and prioritising ideas based on their potential impact and practicality.
4. **Lead by Example**: Demonstrate the value of creativity through successful projects and positive outcomes. Lead by example and show your commitment to fostering a creative culture.
5. **Maintain Momentum**: Keep the creative spirit alive through regular workshops, team-building activities, and continuous learning. Remind your team that creativity is an ongoing journey and encourage a culture of curiosity and exploration.

Conclusion

Creativity is a powerful force that can drive innovation, solve problems, and achieve remarkable success. James's journey demonstrates the transformative impact of embracing creative thinking and fostering a creative culture. By implementing creative processes, fostering a supportive environment, balancing creativity with practicality, leading by example, and maintaining momentum, you can unlock the full potential of creativity in your personal and professional life. Embrace creativity as a valuable asset and let it guide you towards a successful and fulfilling future.

Case Study: "The Creative Connection"

Enhancing personal relationships through creativity can lead to deeper, more meaningful connections. By applying creative thinking to how we interact with others, we can strengthen bonds, improve communication, and make relationships more fulfilling. In this case study, we will explore how one individual used creativity to transform their personal relationships, leading to a more enriched and connected life.

Background

Emily, a marketing manager in her mid-thirties, was known for her professional success but struggled to maintain close personal relationships. She often felt disconnected from her friends and family, finding it difficult to communicate her feelings and make time for meaningful interactions. Emily realised that her relationships were suffering and that she needed to find a new approach to reconnect with the important people in her life.

The Realisation

Emily's realisation came during a team-building retreat organised by her company. One of the activities involved creating vision boards, where participants visualised their personal and professional goals. As Emily worked on her vision board, she noticed that many of her goals were centred around building stronger relationships. This insight prompted her to reflect on how she could apply her creative skills to enhance her personal life.

Inspired by this realisation, Emily decided to approach her relationships with the same creativity she used in her marketing career. She began researching ways to incorporate creative thinking into her interactions with friends and family, hoping to foster deeper connections and improve communication.

Creative Communication

Emily started by focusing on creative communication. She realised that her usual conversations were often superficial and lacked depth. To change this, she began introducing new topics and asking open-ended questions that encouraged meaningful discussions. Instead of the typical "How was your day?" she asked questions like "What's something that inspired you recently?" or "What are you passionate about right now?"

To make her communication more engaging, Emily also started writing letters and notes to her loved ones. She found that taking the time to express her thoughts and feelings in writing helped her communicate more effectively. These personalised messages showed her friends and family that she cared and valued their relationships. The responses she received were overwhelmingly positive, with many expressing appreciation for the effort and thoughtfulness.

Additionally, Emily explored creative ways to stay in touch with her loved ones. She started using voice messages, video calls, and even sending small handmade gifts. These gestures added a personal touch to her communication and helped bridge the gap when face-to-face interactions weren't possible. By being creative in how she communicated, Emily was able to strengthen her connections and foster a deeper sense of intimacy.

Planning Unique Experiences

To further enhance her relationships, Emily began planning unique experiences with her friends and family. She realised that shared activities could create lasting memories and bring people closer together. Instead of the usual dinners and coffee dates, Emily organised creative outings and events that catered to the interests of her loved ones.

One of her first initiatives was a surprise picnic for her best friend, Sarah. Knowing that Sarah loved nature and photography, Emily chose a scenic spot and packed a basket with Sarah's favourite foods. She also brought along a disposable camera for them to capture their day together. The picnic was a huge success, and Sarah appreciated the effort Emily had put into making it special. This experience not only strengthened their friendship but also inspired Sarah to plan a creative outing in return.

Emily also organised themed dinner parties for her family, where each member contributed a dish related to the theme. These dinners became a fun tradition that everyone looked forward to, providing an opportunity for the family to bond and enjoy each other's company. By planning unique experiences, Emily was able to create a sense of excitement and anticipation in her relationships, making them more dynamic and fulfilling.

Creative Problem-Solving in Relationships

Every relationship faces challenges, and Emily realised that applying creative problem-solving could help navigate these difficulties. When disagreements or misunderstandings arose, she approached them with an open mind and a willingness to find innovative solutions. Instead of focusing on the problem, Emily encouraged collaborative brainstorming to identify potential resolutions.

For instance, when Emily and her partner, David, faced a recurring issue of balancing work and personal time, they decided to tackle it creatively. They brainstormed various solutions and eventually came up with the idea of "date nights." Every week, they set aside one evening dedicated to each other, free from work-related distractions. They took turns planning these date nights, which included activities like cooking together, watching a movie, or going for a walk. This approach not only addressed their issue but also added an element of fun and creativity to their relationship.

Emily also applied creative problem-solving with her friends. When a disagreement arose within her friend group about where to go for their annual holiday, Emily suggested a voting system where everyone could propose and vote on destinations anonymously. This fair and democratic approach helped resolve the conflict and ensured that everyone's preferences were considered. By using creativity to solve problems, Emily was able to navigate challenges effectively and maintain harmony in her relationships.

Celebrating Achievements and Milestones

Emily realised that celebrating achievements and milestones creatively could add a special touch to her relationships. Instead of simply acknowledging birthdays or anniversaries, she put effort into making these occasions memorable. Personalised celebrations showed her loved ones that she truly cared and valued their achievements.

For her parents' anniversary, Emily organised a surprise party and created a scrapbook filled with photos and memories from their years together. The effort she put into collecting these memories and crafting the scrapbook made the celebration deeply meaningful for her parents. They were touched by the thoughtfulness and creativity behind the gift, and it became a cherished keepsake.

Emily also celebrated her friends' achievements in creative ways. When her friend Alex completed a marathon, Emily surprised him with a personalised medal and a custom playlist of his favourite songs. These thoughtful gestures not only celebrated Alex's achievement but also showed her support and pride in his accomplishment. By celebrating milestones creatively, Emily was able to deepen her connections and make her loved ones feel appreciated.

Fostering Shared Interests

Emily understood that cultivating shared interests was crucial for building strong relationships. Engaging in activities that both parties enjoyed provided opportunities for quality time and deeper connections. She made an effort to discover and nurture shared interests with her friends and family.

With her partner, David, Emily explored various hobbies they could enjoy together. They took up gardening, which became a relaxing and rewarding activity that they both looked forward to. Working on their garden together allowed them to bond over a shared interest and create something beautiful. They also took cooking classes, which not only improved their culinary skills but also provided a fun and collaborative experience.

Emily also discovered new interests with her friends. She joined a book club with Sarah, where they could discuss their favourite books and explore new genres. This shared interest strengthened their friendship and gave them a common topic to connect over. Emily also participated in a local art class with her friend Mia, which allowed them to express their creativity and support each other's artistic growth. By fostering shared interests, Emily was able to create lasting bonds based on mutual enjoyment and collaboration.

Expressing Gratitude Creatively

Expressing gratitude is a powerful way to strengthen relationships, and Emily found that doing so creatively made her expressions of thanks even more impactful. She made it a habit to regularly show her appreciation in thoughtful and unique ways.

Emily started a tradition of writing gratitude letters to her loved ones. These letters detailed the specific reasons she was grateful for each person and the positive impact they had on her life. She delivered these letters on special occasions or simply when she felt the need to express her appreciation. The recipients were often moved by the sincerity and effort behind the letters, which deepened their emotional connection with Emily.

Additionally, Emily created a "gratitude jar" for her family. Each family member could write notes of appreciation and place them in the jar. During family gatherings, they would read the notes together, fostering a sense of love and gratitude within the family. This creative practice became a cherished tradition that brought them closer together. By expressing gratitude creatively, Emily was able to strengthen her relationships and cultivate a positive and supportive environment.

Conclusion

Emily's journey demonstrates the transformative power of creativity in enhancing personal relationships. By applying creative thinking to communication, planning unique experiences, solving problems, celebrating achievements, fostering shared interests, and expressing gratitude, she was able to build deeper, more meaningful connections with her loved ones. Emily's story highlights that creativity is not just a professional asset but also a valuable tool for enriching our personal lives. By embracing creativity in your relationships, you can foster stronger bonds, improve communication, and create lasting memories that bring joy and fulfilment to both you and your loved ones.

24

Creative Play: Fun Activities to Spark Your Imagination

Creativity is a vital component of personal and professional success. It enables us to solve problems, innovate, and express ourselves. However, fostering creativity isn't always about hard work; it can also be a lot of fun! Engaging in playful activities can stimulate your imagination and unlock new ideas. In this chapter, we will explore a variety of enjoyable activities designed to boost your creativity. These activities are simple, accessible, and perfect for anyone looking to tap into their creative potential.

1. Brainstorming with a Twist

Brainstorming is a classic technique for generating ideas, but it can be made even more effective with a playful twist. Instead of the usual brainstorming session, try using random word association. This technique involves writing down a random word and then brainstorming how it connects to your problem or project.

For example, if you are trying to come up with a new marketing strategy, you might start with the word "ocean." Think about what the ocean represents: vastness, depth, waves, marine life. How can these concepts inspire your marketing strategy?

Perhaps you could create a campaign that emphasises the vast possibilities of your product or service. This playful approach helps you break free from conventional thinking and explore new avenues.

Another twist on traditional brainstorming is to use props or toys. Gather a collection of random objects, such as toy cars, building blocks, or action figures. Pick an object at random and think about how it can inspire your project. This tactile and visual approach can stimulate your mind in unexpected ways and lead to innovative ideas.

2. Doodling and Drawing

Doodling and drawing are excellent ways to foster creativity, even if you don't consider yourself an artist. These activities engage the right side of your brain, which is responsible for creativity and intuition. By allowing your mind to wander and your hand to move freely, you can unlock new ideas and perspectives.

Set aside time each day for doodling or drawing. You don't need any special skills or materials; a simple pen and paper will do. Start with random shapes and lines, and see where your imagination takes you. You might be surprised at the images and concepts that emerge from your doodles.

Another fun activity is to create a visual journal. Each day, draw something that represents your thoughts, feelings, or experiences. This practice not only fosters creativity but also provides a visual record of your journey. You can look back at your visual journal for inspiration and insights into your creative process.

3. Storytelling Games

Storytelling is a powerful way to enhance creativity. It encourages you to think imaginatively, develop characters, and create compelling narratives. Storytelling games can be played alone or with others, making them versatile and enjoyable.

One popular storytelling game is "Story Cubes." This game involves rolling a set of dice with different images on each side. Use the images that appear to create a story. The randomness of the dice forces you to think on your feet and come up with creative connections between the images. This game is great for groups, as each person can contribute to the story, building on each other's ideas.

Another fun storytelling activity is to write a collaborative story. Start by writing a sentence or two, then pass the paper to someone else to continue the story. Keep passing the paper until you have a complete narrative. This collaborative approach can lead to unexpected and delightful stories, as each person's unique perspective adds to the creativity of the final product.

4. Mind Mapping

Mind mapping is a visual technique that helps organise and connect ideas. It starts with a central concept, from which related ideas branch out in all directions. This method mimics the way our brains naturally think, making it easier to see relationships and patterns between different ideas.

To create a mind map, start with a central idea or problem in the middle of a blank page. Draw branches from the central idea, each representing a related concept or solution. Add sub-branches to explore each concept further. Use colours, images, and symbols to make the mind map more engaging and memorable.

Mind mapping can be used for various purposes, such as planning a project, brainstorming ideas, or organising your thoughts. It encourages both linear and non-linear thinking, enabling you to explore different angles and connections. By visually mapping out your ideas, you can gain new insights and develop more comprehensive solutions.

5. Role-Playing and Improvisation

Role-playing and improvisation are excellent ways to foster creativity, as they require you to think quickly and adapt to new situations. These activities can be both fun and educational, providing valuable insights into different perspectives and scenarios.

One way to incorporate role-playing into your routine is through improvisational theatre games. These games involve creating spontaneous scenes based on prompts or scenarios. For example, you might be given a situation where you are a detective interviewing suspects, and you have to come up with questions and responses on the spot. These games encourage you to think creatively and work collaboratively with others.

Another role-playing activity is to imagine yourself in different roles related to your project or problem. For example, if you are developing a new product, imagine yourself as a potential customer, a competitor, or an investor. How would each perspective view your product? What concerns or opportunities might they see? This exercise can help you gain a deeper understanding of your project and identify new angles for innovation.

6. Creative Writing Exercises

Creative writing is a fantastic way to stimulate your imagination and explore new ideas. You don't need to be a professional writer to benefit from these exercises; they are designed to unlock your creativity and improve your storytelling skills.

One simple exercise is freewriting. Set a timer for 10-15 minutes and write continuously without worrying about grammar, spelling, or punctuation. The goal is to let your thoughts flow freely and capture whatever comes to mind. Freewriting can help you overcome writer's block and generate new ideas.

Another creative writing activity is to write from different perspectives. Choose a common object, such as a tree or a coffee cup, and write a story from its point of view. How does it perceive the world? What experiences has it had? This exercise encourages you to think outside the box and develop unique narratives.

7. Music and Movement

Music and movement are powerful tools for fostering creativity. Engaging with music, whether through listening, playing an instrument, or dancing, can stimulate your brain and enhance your mood. These activities encourage you to express yourself and explore new forms of creativity.

Create a playlist of your favourite songs and take a break to dance or move to the music. Let your body move freely and intuitively, without worrying about how you look. This physical expression can release tension and spark new ideas. Dancing can also improve your mood and energy levels, making it easier to approach creative tasks with enthusiasm.

If you play a musical instrument, set aside time each day to experiment with new sounds and compositions. Allow yourself to play without any specific goal in mind, just for the joy of creating music. This freeform approach can lead to unexpected and inspiring musical discoveries.

8. Exploring Nature

Spending time in nature is a wonderful way to boost creativity. The natural environment provides endless inspiration, and the change of scenery can help clear your mind and reduce stress. Activities like hiking, gardening, or simply sitting in a park can stimulate your senses and enhance your creative thinking.

Take a nature walk and bring a notebook or sketchpad with you. Observe the details around you, such as the colours of the leaves, the patterns of the bark, or the sounds of birds. Capture these observations through sketches or written descriptions. This practice can help you see the world with fresh eyes and find inspiration in the beauty of nature.

Gardening is another creative activity that connects you with nature. Planting flowers, vegetables, or herbs allows you to engage with the natural world and create something beautiful. Gardening can be a meditative practice that fosters patience and mindfulness, enhancing your overall creativity.

9. Crafting and DIY Projects

Crafting and DIY projects are hands-on activities that encourage you to create something tangible. These activities can range from simple crafts, like making greeting cards, to more complex projects, like building furniture. Crafting engages your imagination and problem-solving skills, as you design and execute your creations.

Choose a crafting project that interests you and gather the necessary materials. Follow instructions or create your own design, and enjoy the process of bringing your idea to life. Crafting can be a relaxing and satisfying activity that provides a sense of accomplishment. It also allows you to experiment with different techniques and materials, fostering your creativity.

DIY projects can be both practical and creative. For example, repurposing old furniture or creating home decor items can improve your living space while allowing you to express your creativity. These projects often require problem-solving and ingenuity, as you figure out how to transform your ideas into reality.

10. Collaboration and Group Activities

Collaboration is a powerful way to enhance creativity, as it brings together diverse perspectives and ideas. Group activities, whether with friends, family, or colleagues, can inspire you to think differently and develop new concepts. Collaborative creativity encourages communication, teamwork, and mutual support.

Organise a group brainstorming session for a project or problem. Encourage everyone to share their ideas openly and build on each other's suggestions. The synergy of the group can lead to innovative solutions that you might not have thought of on your own. Collaborative brainstorming can also strengthen relationships and foster a sense of community.

Another group activity is to participate in a creative workshop or class. Whether it's a painting class, a writing workshop, or a dance lesson, learning and creating together can be a fun and inspiring experience. Group activities provide opportunities to learn from others, gain new skills, and explore different forms of creativity.